THE SOURCEBOOK
FOR WOMEN WHO CREATE

Edited by

Gail Adams
Martha Miles
Linda Yoder

er for Women's Studies
Virginia University
vn, West Virginia

Design by Rosemary Serian
Multimedia painting on cover by Diane Schwenker
Printing by Fairmont Printing Company, Fairmont, West Virginia
Funded in part by a grant from the Humanities Foundation of West Virginia

Acknowledgements:
The Real Sources

In the preparation of this edition we have had more help than brief acknowledgements can describe. Three writers in particular gave expert advice and unstinting encouragement: Maggie Anderson, Kathleen Diehl, and Devon McNamara. We also thank those who carefully read the first edition (*Masks, Myths and Marmalade: A Sourcebook on Women and Creativity,* 1984) and gave thoughtful criticism: Mildred Atkins, Carol Bryan, Marilyn Enslow, Winston Fuller, Louise Lamar-Fuller, Martha Manning, Lotus MacDowell, Pat Penn and Carroll Wilkinson.

To those earlier contributing authors who provided much of the text used in shaping this revision, we are grateful: Linda Morningstar for research on the photography section, Katherine Payne for shaping the responses of the homemaker-artists, and Stephanie Pratt for her excellent bibliography in classical music. We also thank Andrea Soccorsi for her good cheer in the time-consuming task of verifying references and sources.

Our deep thanks go to Jennie Dinsmore, whose enthusiasm and support in all phases of the first design helped us to believe we had an idea worth developing. And to others who responded to pleas for help, for consultation, for information, we thank you — Mary Lucille DeBerry, Beatrice deVegvar, Ann Osman, and Margaret Stilwell.

Jessie Herrera and Judy Mossberg of West Virginia University Women's Studies Center were unfailingly helpful in guiding us through financial and administrative labyrinths, while David Grimm, student assistant at the Center, deserves a special thanks for cheerfully and knowledgeably turning our typed pages into organized and computerized prose.

The West Virginia Department of Culture and History eased our way tremendously throughout the life of this project. We especially thank Sherry Hairston-Hughes, Mike Keller, Sandy Keller, Rebecca Stelling, and Frances Whited, who were courteous and accommodating, giving us access to the collections and helping us locate materials and people.

And because this book had its genesis in the 1984 Conference on Women and Creativity, the editors are indebted to Margaret Lorince and Sharon Goodman and their entire committee for providing a source of creative energy for so many women. By their enthusiasm and dedication, they encouraged us at our task. And to Sharon especially, whose hand in this work was felt from idea to appearance, for everything you provided us with, from supper to critique — thank you, Sharon.

And to the Humanities Foundation of West Virginia, and especially its Executive Director, Charles Daugherty, we want to say "thank you," first, for significant financial support, but more important, for the

3

confidence shown to us for the success of this project.

For financial support we also cite with thanks:

The Women's Information Center, Inc. of Morgantown
Council for Women's Concerns, West Virginia University
First Federal Savings and Loan of Morgantown
Tri-State Printing, Steubenville, Ohio
The Dominion Post
Dorsey and Kiger Realtors
Barry's Office Service
GARO — Tomlinson Collection
Superior Photo
D/P Inc., Photographics
Elizabeth Mason Martin, Attorney at Law
Suncrest Travel Service
Rogers' Interiors
Sue and Dennis Overman
Erma Edwards
Kathleen Diehl
Susan Williams

Grateful acknowledgement is made for permission to reprint the following:

Maggie Anderson. "Sitting There: The Discipline of Writing" and "Art and Accident." "Art and Accident" was originally published in slightly different form in *West Virginia Art News* (vol. 3, no. 2, May-June 1981) and "Sitting There" in vol. 3, no. 3, July-August 1981. By permission of the author.

"Sometimes Inside Us." Copyright 1984. By permission of the author.

Christine Beregi. "I Am." First published in *American Poetry Anthology,* vol. 2, no. 2 (Santa Cruz, CA: American Poetry Association) August 1983. *Collecting Myself: A Journal* is unpublished. Both by permission of the author.

Betty Donley Harris. "I Write in Order to Live." By permission of the author. First appeared in *CALYX, A Journal of Art and Literature by Women,* vol. 9, no. 2 & 3, *Women and Aging Anthology.*

Karen Mackay. "West Virginia Woman." Copyright 1982, lyrics from *West Virginia Woman.* Used by permission of the author.

Devon McNamara. "Finding the Marmalade." Copyright 1984. By permission of the author.

Carol Ann Shinn Schweiker. "Today the Sheets." By permission of the author.

The West Virginia Department of Culture and History for "Monstrance," the mixed-media painting on the cover by Diane Schwenker, which won the Governor's Award in 1983 and is a part of the West Virginia Permanent Collection.

●

Preface

Judith Stitzel

There is no other book like this one. This book would not be possible without all that came before. These statements, both true, encompass the miracle of creativity.

Who has not felt herself to be an artist? Who has not ridden that wave of certainty and clarity that signals creation? No one, I would venture. But who has then been able to say to herself, "For this new work, this new idea, image, sound, shape, I praise myself and count on care from those who cherish it"? Not many, I'm afraid, regardless of our class, or race or culture. For as Tillie Olsen, Virginia Woolf and Alice Walker have etched into our consciousness, for a women to be an artist in a woman-doubting world requires a proclamation of faith and love—in women, in oneself as woman—that challenges the ages.

This book, like the conference it grew out of, is such a proclamation. The book, like the conference, was a gift fashioned by women for women, a gift of our best selves to ourselves. It combines the practical and specific with the spiritual and the speculative. Conference planners and Sourcebook editors were influenced by Virginia Woolf's profound recognition that while the creative impulse may not be rooted in the material, fruition demands the congenial loam of receptivity.

The flourishing of women artists and the artist in all women has been cruelly restricted. We have been denied access to education, to information, to money, and to support. We have been pulled apart by impossible choices— between creativity and parenthood, between security and discovery, and between intimacy and growth.

This is changing, not by itself and not easily, but through bold and caring enterprises like this one. This book is a matrix of connections and a focus of energy. Sharon Goodman brought the idea to the Creativity Conference Steering Committee, offering it tentatively at first but proudly and sure of its magic. Gail Adams carried the idea boldly through the conference planning, stretching it, getting more and more people involved, challenging people into response. Linda Yoder and Martha Miles looked at the first edition, knew it was good, knew that with energy and love there could be more and that we deserved it. Sharon, Gail, Linda, Martha— these are the people I knew best; each of them could name others they depended on ... and each of them ... and each of you... And so it goes— sources and resources, strength feeding strength, unending.

The Sourcebook is a first for the Center for Women's Studies at West Virginia University and we are very proud. It embodies what we stand for— the empowering of women and, through that empowering, the enrichment of life. There is no other book like this one. The book would not be possible without all that came before.

Sometimes Inside Us

for Sharon Goodman

Sometimes inside us
like a forest at dusk
there are trees that move in the wind.

Or, as inside a house
there may be only a view of trees
from an attic window
the orange leaves and black limbs
barely breathing as cars pass beneath.
They are framed by the white wood house next door
and streaked with grey sky.

The view is through a small green pane,
the curtains pushed back,
where sometimes she stands
and notices the morning scent
her son's shoulder left on her palms.

Sometimes inside us
it remains October
though a swirl of white wind starts up.

What holds us steady
is the roof of the attic,
the squeaks in the floorboards
and the dark walls.
We stay for the sake of the bannisters,
the sound of the rain in the street.

What holds us steady
is the roots of these trees
as we imagine them held
in solid earth
as rich and black as perpendicular lines.

And we are held together by each other's hands.
What holds us together is each other's hands.

Contents

Art and Accident

Maggie Anderson

Accidental discoveries are crucial to the making of art. Inexplicable happenings—the word that suddenly appears everywhere we look, or the slight shift in light that will prompt us to see something which has been there all along but gone unnoticed—are at the core of the mysterious origins of poetry, painting, music, or dance. The element of chance involved even in the lives of people who do not call themselves artists cannot be discounted. But for those of us who do call ourselves artists, the accidents and the seemingly accidental repetitions of our lives hold a particular responsibility.

Maggie Anderson

Accident in art is not exactly like the hypothetical monkeys with the typewriters who may eventually come up with *Richard III*. Certainly, in the case of those monkeys (if there are enough of them, and enough typewriters) the odds are increased that they might, one day, type up something intelligible; they might reinvent language. But the responsibility for the artist when faced with apparent accident lies in knowing what to do with the miracles, the strangeness that chance throws up.

Most of us have had the experience of finding a particular word, or a particular idea, suddenly mentioned or appearing in our lives with great frequency after, seemingly, never having been there before. A woman in a workshop of mine recently referred to this as the "scuppernong phenomenon." She got the term from a friend of hers who had encountered the word "scuppernong," a type of grape, no fewer than ten separate times in the space of a week. Until this week of scuppernong saturation, she had never (as far as she knew) heard the word before.

Carl Jung called this phenomenon "synchronicity," the idea that the world will throw up for us what we need. Jung says, "When coincidences pile up in this way one cannot help but be impressed by them—for the greater the number of terms in such a series, or the more unusual its character, the more improbable it becomes." "Scuppernong" is certainly unusual; ten times in a week is certainly frequent.

The particular task for an artist is to know what to do with a synchronous term like "scuppernong" when it occurs. For a writer, the sudden appearance of an unusual word is no small matter. For a painter the impact (and the mandate) might come from particular repetitions of shapes or colors. Georgia O'Keeffe has spoken about collecting the pelvic bones of animals in the desert, a "scuppernong" gift in her life, knowing that someday she would know what to do with them: "I do not remember picking up the first one but I remember from when I first noticed them always knowing I would one day be painting them."

Recently, I found the word "palimpsest" (the term for an erased tablet on which new writing has been added over the faint image of what's been erased). I came across the word in three different places in one day. It is an unusual enough word that, for a writer, its repetitious appearance seems to demand that something be done with it.

"Palimpsest," however, is not the sort of word one uses often in a poem. I knew that, once used, its possibilities would be exhausted in my work, at least for a long time. I spent several weeks trying to decide if I was to write a new poem about "palimpsest," write only one line with an image of palimpsest in it, or try to smuggle the word into a line of an old poem that might seem to need some literary panache.

The solution came to me much later, with as much suddenness as the original word. I had a three-part poem I had been working with for months. I considered the poem finished, but it had no title. One day, as I was rereading the poem, I realized that all three parts were, in a metaphorical way, a description of palimpsest. My found word became my title and one additional line in the poem.

The poet Seamus Heaney comments on accident in poetry in this way, injecting a cautionary note: "A poem always has elements of accident about it, which can be made the subject of inquest afterward, but there is always a risk in conducting your own inquest: you might begin to believe the coroner in yourself rather than put your trust in the one who is capable of the accident." For the artist, it is more important to know what to do with the accidents and how to increase their frequency of occurrence than to know what might have caused them to occur.

The synchronicity of words like "scuppernong" or "palimpsest," or the unknown but deeply felt significance of the shapes of the pelvic bones of animals are accidental occurrences that may come to anyone. Accepting artistic responsibility means knowing where to go with these mysterious gifts. What teaches that is practice, vigilance, and lots of mistaken use. The time to get ready for accident in art, as in life, is when it is not occuring—all those low, slow, uninspired days when words like "palimpsest" do not boom down from the sky.

The most frustrating thing about these kinds of accidents, in fact, is that they are not always forthcoming. Whole years may go by with no miraculous accidental discovery. There are, however, certain things that artists can do to make themselves more receptive to accidents, to be ready for them should they happen by, and to provide the right environment for them to occur.

(1) *Cultivate laziness:* Accidents need room to roam around in. People often say that their most inspired thoughts come to them in the bathtub, or right before they fall asleep. At those times, the body (and the mind) are relaxed enough to drift over the plethora of accidental connections in the universe. Artists whose lives are eaten away with the struggle to earn a living at something other than their art (i.e., most artists) have particular difficulty with this. If you have only evenings and weekends in which to write, there will be a sort of insistence with yourself that the precious hours you have snatched can only be spent actually writing.

May Sarton, in her journal *Recovering*, comments on a valuable lesson she learned from Muriel Rukeyser about loafing: ". . . loafing is not a crime . . . to lie around reading magazines and appearing to do nothing can be a very good idea . . . . Being 'active,' 'doing something' may be an escape from loafing for when one loafs, the imagination springs into being and all kinds of unexpected things may happen in the psyche." C. Day Lewis puts it even more directly: ". . . like most budding artists I had a great capacity for laziness . . . I needed, without knowing why, those times of apparent inaction, apathy almost, when the mind is passive like a net swayed by deep-sea currents, taking in whatever comes its way." Cultivating laziness, making the space and time to loaf, can provide the right climate for artistic accidents to begin to manifest themselves.

(2) *Save things:* Joseph Cornell, the great artistic collector, said, "Everything can be used—but of course one doesn't know it at the time. How does one know what a certain object will tell another?" Collecting objects, or scraps of paper, writing down quotes, taking photographs for no "reason" except that they feel important, are all artists' characteristics. A writing group I worked with in Marshall County, West Virginia decided that all one really needs to be a writer is a drawer—full of stuff, slips of paper, newspaper clippings, notes, words, pictures—that will one day turn to art. Painters or sculptors often collect shells, or pieces of wood, or bones. These idiosyncratic collections of things provide the materials for the accidents of art to begin to be realized. One day, if you have saved carefully, you will look at your stack of papers and they will have begun to form a story, or a poem. One day, a painter might realize that the shapes which have been an obsession of years are all alike, connected, in ways he or she had not realized before. Georgia O'Keeffe describes this occult process: "I find that I have painted my life—things happening in my life—without knowing. After painting the shell and shingle many times, I did a misty landscape of the mountain across the lake, and the mountain became the shape of the—mountain I saw out my window, the shingle on the on the table in my room. I did not notice that they were alike for a long time after they were painted."

(3) *Pay close attention during personal crisis:* The emotional intensity that accompanies periods of personal crisis in our lives increases the likelihood of productive accident. Many people have noticed, at times of crisis, that certain psychic qualities are enhanced—instances of *deja vu* and precognitive dreams may be more frequent; we may seem to know what people are thinking before they speak. Artistic creation is, in many ways, like estrasensory awareness. At times of crisis in our lives artistic recognitions may be heightened as well. Usually the hub of a personal crisis is the worst possible time to make art, but it is perhaps the best time to make notes, to save things we find interesting and intriguing, and to remember what happens. These are the materials from which we will, later, create.

(4) *Take risks and make mistakes:* One of the biggest killers of creativity is what the poet Louise Bogan has called "the knife of the perfectionist," the terror of mistakes in art and in life. The fear of taking risks (emotional and personal, as well as what are more generally defined as "artistic" risks), the fear of being found "silly" or "wrong," closes the doors to accident and chance discovery. If we fear that turning a painting sideways, or covering it all with blue paint, will be silly, we will cut off a possibility for creative accident. If we fear breaking metric pattern in a poem, just to see what might happen, we will have walled off the "scuppernong phenomena" and the opportunity for words and sounds to reveal themselves to us in new ways. The accidents of art can only reveal themselves to us if we are willing to dare being found silly or wrong, to break the rules, to attempt what seems, perhaps even to us, outrageous.

The poet Adrienne Rich says, "Poems are like dreams, in them we put what we don't know we know." But this is only possible if we allow ourselves to be open to the possibilities of accident, chance connections in our lives, so that we can begin to learn the things about ourselves and others that art can teach us. The artist's task is to create a life and an environment that leaves room for accidents to occur. The artist's responsibility is to use these accidents carefully and intelligently so that, as Paul Klee says, our art can be "the secretly perceived made visible."

The responsibility for the artist
when faced with an apparent accident
lies in knowing what to do
with the miracles.

—Maggie Anderson

Eloise Tomei "Rosetta"

11

Two-Dimensional Art:

I Found I Did Have Talent

Sharon Goodman and Sharon Santos

Jan Griffin

Mitzi Kellogg

There are as many different ways of becoming artists as there are women willing to share their experiences in doing so. The central thread within the women and their stories, abbreviated versions of which follow, appears to be their commitment and determination to pursue their art and to define their talent. While some knew they were artists from an early age, others found it a long period before discovering their real bent. Moreover, some of these women had extensive training and professional degrees, yet others taught themselves or found classes, workshops, or help when they needed it. What made the difference was that they somehow did not give up on themselves or their talent.

Discovering the Talent

Ruth Blackwell Rogers of Kerens says, "From the time I was seven years old I knew I would be an artist. . . I was encouraged by my family. But it was not until college that began to work seriously. There I studied under Elliott Twery and realized that I wanted to do more than copy the way light strikes an object." And like Ruth, Nancy Taylor, of Gauley Bridge, associates her art with her childhood. "I have always painted, drawn, built, and created. My childhood was isolated somewhat and the loneliness was probably the most powerful influence on the development of these interests—to create your own fun mentality, I suppose. I attribute my talents to a God-given hand-eye coordination and unquenchable curiosity about everything visual, which encouraged unusual observations and attitude developments. Translation: a lonely kid turns to nature and art and is surprised to discover by third grade that this talent made me see things differently."

For many women the discovery of their talent was interrupted by a commitment to rearing a family or assisting a husband in business. Rosalie Atkins married young, had children, and started a business with her husband. She says, "As I got locked into a routine of managing a business, rearing children, and running a home I found myself with a need to fulfill my educational and emotional needs. I had been a good student and felt I should continue my education. My father, unfortunately, felt art a waste of time and therefore channeled all my talents and interests in other directions, languages and math, for example. In 1951 when I finally went back to college, I had already started to think about a major in art. I enrolled in Mason College of Music and Fine Art, first in part-time classes. Well, a new world opened up for me. I found I did have talent, and it was endless the work I did."

Helen Bratt's story is similar. Her formal art training was interrupted when she married and had children. As she says of herself, "When my older two children were four years and one year, I started taking art classes one night a week. This went on for seven years or so. Several of the other art students with whom I studied are still working with me in various art groups. So I would encourage mothers who can't find the time to create to join an art class and make the time."

Elizabeth McClain of Morgantown may best sum up how early discovery of talent helped her establish and define her commitment to her art. Crediting her early and good art training with helping her combine a family and an art studio, McClain says, "My parents saw I liked to draw and got me to a teacher very early. At age 14, I was painting nudes, shocked to my eyeballs, but if I hadn't had that kind of training, I would never have been able to have and bring up six children, painting and drawing through it all. I found time to be in my studio for some hours every day, more or less as family needs came and went. It was "what mother did," and we all accepted it as normal. It's a risk venture to be sure; no one can foretell whether it will work for you or not, but at least for me, it was well worth the effort. Family pressure does get less as time goes on, and time widens out beautifully."

Nurturing It

Once the women artists determined both their talent and their commitment to it, most of them revealed that it was vital to nurture and pursue that talent. Classes and workshops, they agreed, are not a necessity but they help. They can stimulate. They can provide professional criticism. And they can provide a peer group. Ultimately, however, each individual must work through to her own vision.

Four Charleston artists write of the place of these forces in their development. Nancy Thompson Gunnoe, says, "I would tell anyone interested in becoming a painter to study or take classes at a college if possible. Don't waste your time or money on anything but the best education. If I were starting now in art, I would also look into the opportunities of traveling abroad on tours, which are often offered by many of the colleges." Anne Shreve, says, "I took every art course offered and private lessons as well. The last couple of years I've studied a month each year in New York. But mostly, I consider myself self-taught. I think most artists are." Jan Griffin, also credits workshops and further training as necessary for her artistic endeavors. She recalls, "I take every workshop related, even distantly, to what I'm doing. I've been included three times in the New Masters Workshops at the Huntington Galleries, where I found many people as much involved in problem solving as I." Others also mentioned how valuable were the New Masters Workshops at the Huntington Galleries.

Paula Clendenin applied for and received a fellowship to the MacDowell Colony in New England and a three-month residency in Vence, France, as a Karolyi Foundation Fellow. "My career in art thus far," recounts Paula, "has been like crossing a wide creek full of scattered stepping stones—so many to choose from. Some turn out to be weak or point you in the wrong direction; others take you to the beautiful and fulfilling spot, leading to still further aspirations. It's exciting. It's challenging, and it's full of surprises."

Continued growth is a theme of Ellen Elmes of Jewell Ridge. "A self-employed artist as I am has no one to tell her what to do. That fact turns out to be one of the most difficult aspects of my work. You have to push yourself—to continue to grow and get better, to follow disciplined work hours, and to meet deadlines you got yourself into. To be aggressive and have nerve enough to say your're good, to admit to yourself when you're messed up and need to start the work over—these, too, are part of growth." "Expanding artistically," an apt summation, is how Carolyn Sanders-Turner of Beckley describes her own struggles. "It has been a difficult and in many ways lonely struggle. First, the adjustment within our family which includes two children, my work and my role changes, priority differences, time away to get work out in the world, time spent painting, and all the energy it all takes. Next was that it was important for my work to be taken seriously, not as a hobby but real work. Through all this, connections have been established with other artists and professional people, gallery owners, outlets, and shows.

"Having spent the first few years adjusting to these things, *expanding artistically*, learning professional ropes, now in the 12th year the ongoing problem seems to be a fight against lack of challenge and stimulation. Keeping the magic spark of imagination and creativity and growth fresh. Actually, I feel that part of the artistic impasse now is due to too much time spent on business, which really has nothing to do with art. My present solution has been to use this year for experimentation, to spend a month living and studying at the Art Students League in New York."

Rogers says that growth for her meant this: "From the beginning I decided that doing my work—creating in the studio—was more important to me than making a lot of money. My husband's position was similar. So we cultivated ways of living inexpensively while still harmoniously. Country living, communal living for six years, and stopping our work for twelve months to build a house we designed, then adding a studio, have been joint efforts of our family to live in a peaceful atmosphere with rather uncertain and limited resources."

The thing, of course, that often sets women artists apart from men is that the women artists bear and nurture children and keep the house, experiences that most women, artists or not, want to have. The demands are great, but art must be kept alive through the difficult periods. "I find," says Bratt, "that when I concentrate on cleaning the house, I neglect my art; when concentrate on art, I neglect my house." Elizabeth McClain, however, recalls, "Doing dishes, so often I would be looking at a painting. The time spent looking is as imporant as actually putting on paint. I feel more motivated to organize what housework I have if I know I can then have some hours to paint." And Elmes: "Art can become a driving force in a person's life—it is in mine—but this creative force within me is cradled within and nurtured by the love of my family."

"Start every new piece fresh or your work looks stale," is a principle that Sharon Goodman, a Morgantown artist, discovered. "Something my printmaking teacher Will Peterson said is, 'Don't make imitations of yourself.' One week he would praise my work, and the next he would dismiss it saying, 'Imitation of yourself.' He was right—every time I try to repeat a successful formula it doesn't work.

"Sometimes I start with a definite idea, knowing I will most likely wind up with something altogether different from the original idea. Other times I will begin by making a mark and then another mark. And then it continues. I make more marks in answer to the marks. It can be like solving a puzzle with endless possibilities, finding the proper marks that bring it to a suitable conclusion for me.

" 'Drawing is gathering information.' These words changed my entire approach to my work."

THE PAINTING

Paint something old
they say is highly art
an ocean racked with waves
a fleshed-out nude
the irreversible balance
of bottles and pears
a known bridge

Paint something new
that causes itself to be
a purple curve that ends
with 3-D spikes
the perpendicular footprints
of calico cats
on a quilt

Paint something yours
that grows between each stroke
your constant need to cry
today's gray air
the unmistakeable fury
of working alone
that you choose

—Jane Ray Halpin

Painting grows out of a woman's entire life. Rogers says, "Gradually, I have come to paint in series, sometimes continuing a series after several years, sometimes plunging through one in a few months. I prefer to paint in a fairly large size so that the viewer is confronted with an image big enough to fully absorb him or her, to make an impression as powerful as a strong, warm hug." Ellie Schaul of Charleston is constantly striving for new directions. "I could never paint 'the same old thing.' I absorb all the objects and forces around me—this is what I put on paper." Taylor might be speaking for many when she writes, "Personally, I am happiest when working on new innovative techniques which reflect a personal statement. I believe that art is an extension of me."

Many women wrote of the beauty of West Virginia and how it influenced their work. Elmes says, "We live on top of a mountain in West Virginia, and our seclusion and the beauty around us provide the well from which we thrive and from which I paint. So many of my paintings reflect or come from nature because there are endless and infinite relationships and patterns to study there and to wonder about." Shreve says, "Although I've lived in Charleston all my life, I really don't want to be thought of just as an Appalachian artist. I certainly do paint Appalachia, but think I see a different aspect of the area than most people think of when they think of Appalachia. I've never seen a coal mine." However, Paula Clendenin, born and reared in a small coal mining town, thought of West Virginia as a "place to leave." Following graduate school, she worked and traveled all over the country. But after buying an etching press, she knew she needed place to settle and now speaks of West Virginia as "a source of strength and texture in my work."

Artists seek renewal. "Once a year," says Griffin, "I join two or three friends and we spend a week at a state park drawing and painting and refreshing our minds and eyes." For Rogers, "Poets and their work have periodically been an inspiration for me. And more recently, musicians and their music, and mime and dance people and their work have stimulated me perhaps more than other visual artists. Elkins has much music and movement to offer." Elmes says, "My love of creating is one thing. The business of creating is another. When all is said and done, no matter how good an artist knows her work to be, she must enjoy a public response. She must hear a stranger comment on how much her painting means to him/her. There must be communication between the creator and the observer. Artists need to share their expression and receive the response."

Caryl Toth, of Winfield, has found this state congenial to her work. "West Virginia, in general, has been a support network for me. Allied Artists, The Art Store, The Cultural Center, The Art Education Association, the Guild, Penwomen, the universities and all the many artist friends I have throughout the state." To beginners, she says, "work hard—work constantly—meet people—share ideas—keep a journal—see relationships in all that you observe, do, and think. Show your work as much as possible, enter shows which are juried by professionals—never stop growing."

*A lonely kid turns to nature
and art and is surprised to discover
that this talent made me see things
differently.*

—Nancy Taylor

Working It Out

The woman artist must deal with two realities: where she is to paint and how she is to market what she paints. Sanders-Turner works in a studio that was once her garage, after adding a north window, replacing the garage door with three thermal glass doors, tiling the cement floor with adobe tile, painting rafters with a white wash, and heating with electric baseboard heat. "I would love to have a separate space six times larger and separate from the house. The things that are essential are good, natural light and ample, comfortable work space."

Griffin built a 24' x 24' studio attached to her home and perfectly tailored it for her silkscreen needs, including in it work tables, drying lines, fans, dryer, storage cabinets, among other things. "The flooring is rough plywood, not painted but signed by friends and art types with magic marker (a real conversation piece), and the plywood was laid over two by fours 30 inches apart over a cement pad. All of this was done to keep legs and feet from tiring after eight to ten hours a day of standing in one place while screening. I now have a small Sears trampoline that I have set up near the screening area, and while one of the processes is drying, I hop on the trampoline and have a go at 300 jumps. This improves my circulation and isn't bad for my body."

Although Gunnoe does not have a studio, she says, "I usually do watercolor on the kitchen table since it has to be wet down." Taylor believes one's own space to be essential. "Private studio space, even if it's a room corner in your house, provides a necessary place for work and creativity. An absolute necessity! I spent an entire summer and about 54,000 to design and build exactly what I need. The expense is a tax deduction business expense but is well worth the trouble even without this advantage." Lotus MacDowell's solution to the question of studio space is to share. "I have a studio which overlooks downtown Clarksburg, which I share with a woman who teaches art in a local high school. I have it all to myself except for the summer, so have a lot of peace and quiet. I am up two floors in an apartment complex, old with lots of personality and huge windows, so I do not get much traffic in and out. When I looked for the place, I wanted one with a good atmosphere. This place has dark natural woodwork, wood floors, old fireplaces with antique gas inserts and green tiles, bay window in my workroom, large single ones in the others, reasonable rent, and NO COCKROACHES!!

"Wherever my studio is, I like to surround myself with lots of objects and collectibles for things to draw. We both accumulated tons of stuff over the years, so it is really cozy instead of austere. Light is essential to my work and I get southern light, which is not the best, but I supplement it with other lights. I have a complete kitchen so I can cook or keep foods here and even invite prospective clients up for lunch, as well as my husband!"

Bratt, on the other hand, advises not to let the lack of ideal space prevent one from painting. "My present studio is a bedroom converted. My younger sister once brought friends to the small apartment where we lived and said, 'This is Helen's studio; she also lives here.'"

Showing It

Marketing one's paintings, "getting your work out of the studio," as one artist called it, really means marketing oneself. Says Mary Black, Charleston, "As an individual business I am listed as a freelance artist; the name of my business is STUDIO 217." Many give a name to their studios: Artworks, Lotus MacDowell; the Picture Place, Ellen Elmes; Light Impressions, Paula Meadows; Earthform Studio, Nancy Taylor; and The Art Attic, Eloise Tomei. Sanders-Turner explains, "I use my own name but in the past year I also published limited edition prints, so we set up a marketing company for them, WATERMARK PRESS. Taylor recommends using business cards. "I encourage investment in these as they present your business in a professional light."

Artists find that management skills are called for. "I keep thorough complete records," says Griffin. "Each print issued has a page in a notebook. When one of the edition is sold, that name and date is recorded and the amount the customer paid for it. This is your inventory." When her prints are not selling well, says Griffin, "turns to design work and prints notecards for gift shops. "This also serves to keep my name before the art public. I deal with a local printing firm who cuts the stock and orders the envelopes for me."

Tomei, of Morgantown, too designed her own business cards and stationery and "spent literally hours on the phone the first year, making necessary contacts, establishing clientele, developing mailing lists. I still write all my ads and articles which appear in print about "The Art Attic," as well as design all our educational programs and promotional ideas."

Artists, like most of us, must also deal with insurance. About that issue, Taylor reveals, "I regret that I cannot afford proper insurance on all my work. Losses of fine art pieces which have not been properly evaluated by good sources result in losses for which only materials can be claimed. For example, the last copy of a print which had won the $1,000 Award of Excellence in a WV Juried Exhibition and which was uninsured was destroyed when a small child knocked it over in a bank exhibit. In spite of honors and established selling price of $200, all that was claimable was the cost of glass and one sheet of paper."

Four Charleston artists, Anne Shreve, Susan Poffenberger, Jan Griffin, and Helen Clinton, loaded up a van with samples of their work and explored Washington, D.C., for possible outlets. They were featured in a Washington exhibit entitled "Three Painters and a Printmaker," and the contacts led to additional gallery showings. Said Shreve, "I feel it is very important to the artist to visit the galleries one is considering approaching, to become acquainted with the owners and to make inquiries about their financial stability and their general treatment of the artists they represent. The main consideration, however, is the other work that a gallery carries—the quality, the other artists, for example, also storage space and how paintings are cared for when not hanging. A good gallery is much like a good publisher—they pay all, or practically all, expenses, making their money solely on commission from sales. The combined interest makes the artist submit only her best work and makes the gallery work hard on sales and promotion of the work and reputation."

Other Charleston artists formed their own gallery, "Gallery Eleven," a co-op, which Mary Black writes, "was established nine years ago; we advertise in the local paper, print brochures, and occasionally send invitations for openings. It is necessary for the members to subsidize the business. Anyone going into this type of business must look forward with patience for slow growth. Our shop is small and we would like a larger space, but downtown rents are very high."

Agents are yet another possibility. Rogers writes, "I have a couple of agents in three states who do pretty well selling my paintings. But I've gone through three or four poor agents."

Getting your work out of the studio, matted, and framed is a good experience. If you're not ready to show in a prominent gallery, consider the possibility of a restaurant or library exhibit; it is advantageous to see your work hanging on unfamiliar walls. It also gives others a chance to see your work. Concurring is Schaul, who says, "Some day I look forward to seeing all my work together in one space. Just to review phases that have led me to today." From Taylor, "My most successful contacts are out-of-state friends who have put me in contact with interior decorators or galleries."

Another excellent outlet is The Artists' Register at the Cultural Center in Charleston. Artists submitting slides to the Register receive a newsletter with valuable information on events, shows, and grants; artists with slides on file may also be considered for exhibitions. Other professional organizations that were recommended are Allied Artists of West Virginia, National League of American Penwomen, WV Artists and Craftsmen Guild, Bara'ka, Tri-State Artists Association, Mercer Art Guild, Southern Watercolor Society, The Studio Group, and The Women's Caucus for Art.

Older now, her children grown, Atkins writes in conclusion, "Art has been very rewarding to me. I'm no longer a Sunday painter. Everything centers around my painting, my exhibitions, my galleries. We follow art in West Virginia and Florida and it's never a dull moment."

Finally, from Tomei, "My decision to establish my own studio/gallery as a small business was motivated by the fact that I had decided to stay in Morgantown and could only find part-time jobs in my field of Fine Arts. With encouragement from family and friends, I decided to open my own business. I'd always been interested in operating an "informal art gallery" and thought that perhaps I'd be able to support my own studio/gallery by offering art lessons to children and adults. I had had a lot of teaching experience and enjoyed it considerably, so I thought I'd try it. As for whether or not it has worked out? I'll be celebrating five years of being in business in June, 1986. I think that speaks for itself."

Clay: I Could Hear the Clay Calling Me

Judy Mattson Reed

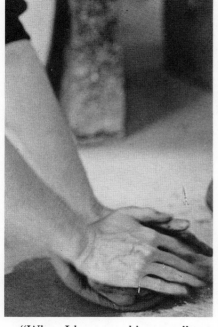

Ever since my childhood, when I discovered a clay pit, clay has been important to me. Over the years, the tactile, sensuous quality of the clay has drawn me. The satisfaction that I get from working on the wheel, seeing the shapes develop from a mound of clay, and realizing I did that with my own hands rewards me. Opening a glaze kiln is like Christmas morning. Clay has been my benefactor and has sustained me through periods of happiness and crisis.

I am a potter and an art teacher at Salem College. Pottery came naturally to me, maybe because my father was a ceramic designer in the glass and pottery industry, and I grew up around the art. I didn't teach pottery at first after earning my M.A. in art education. But being in the college atmosphere, seeing the pottery equipment, I found my love for clay rekindled. I started practicing, reading, attending workshops, and talking to other potters. The joys of teaching are those of seeing my students grow as potters and of learning from them as well.

How it is that a medium becomes for one the means for creative expression presents us with a puzzle as mysterious as the selection of a lover. The women potters with whom I corresponded tried to respond to this question.

"When I began making pots," says Louise Lamar-Fuller of Morgantown, "I used to joke about having to go back to the studio at night because I could hear the clay calling me. But I could hear it calling—it was like falling in love. Over the years that dropped away. Now I go to the studio to do the work because it's a pleasure and a discovery and it's who I am."

"For the first few years after I started working with clay," she remembers, "I thought that choosing clay had been *all* timing. That the time had been right for me to do something new and that just happened to be clay. Now I can remember hearing a potter talking of her work fifteen years before I started and I remember asking, without success, two different women whose pots I'd seen if they would teach me. So the connection with clay seems to have been there even before the right moment arrived." Lamar-Fuller is one of several artists to choose clay after another profession, in her case, teaching English. She learned to make pots at WVU's Craft Shop; within two years, she was its director.

"Like most novice potters," continues Lamar-Fuller, "I started out making my own notebook containing pictures and sketches of pots and other forms that attracted me. At first it was things I saw. Later it became things I think of, ideas, solutions to problems, shapes I dream of. I have to be prepared to get up at 3 a.m. and get it down on paper. What is more demanding by far is the effort of translating pictures and ideas into *things*. 'Translating' is the right word, because just as something is lost (and something gained, perhaps) in moving a

19

poem from Russian or Chinese or Spanish to English, something is always lost or gained in moving an idea into reality. So much perseverence, discipline, learning are required! Perseverence, discipline, learning—sum them up as 'craft.' Craft is the greatest resource. It enables you to do what you imagine. And it carries you when your imagination takes a vacation."

Pam Parziale, who works with her husband Ren in Kearneysville, has a degree in English literature from Colby College, Waterville, Maine. She attended Haystack Mountain School of Crafts, apprenticed under Vally Possony, a studio potter, and attended Penland School of Crafts.

Parziale writes, "One might say I had a late start for a career in the arts. It was significant for me, however, as I made a concentrated effort to overcome the traditional stereotypes of a craftsworker."

Another potter who changed careers for pottery is Marcia Springston of Forest Hill. "It had never occurred to me to be an artist as a profession," says Springston, who has a degree in social psychology. Her first experience with pottery was in a high school independent study program. "After college I was reintroduced to pottery while on vacation in Colorado. I started taking night classes in pottery while working at a historical museum which featured glass-blowing, weaving, and clay, and I got a lot of inspiration for my pots from my work there. Gradually I began purchasing pottery equipment, such as a kiln and a wheel. Pottery was still a hobby, but I was beginning to hope it would be my profession. I wanted to become more proficient in the craft, so I studied ceramics and sculpture for a year."

Springston, who has been blind from birth, speaks of the difficulty of making the choice between pottery and her work in the rehabilitation of the blind. "The latter would make me financially secure, but disappointed that I couldn't succeed at an independent venture. On the other hand, pottery might mean years of struggle ending in failure."

Reverses came often. "I was offered a job teaching Braille when I heard about an opening for an Artist in Residence in MacDowell County. Again I chose pottery."

Many women potters started their pottery interest early and now combine it with teaching. "I have been working with clay off and on for eight years," writes Buffy Point of Morgantown. "After teaching high school and elementary art, I started an MA in art education at Rhode Island School of Design and got so involved in clay that I wanted more study in that area." Point continued her interest in ceramics by obtaining a MFA from WVU and since then has taught and shown her work.

The Life of a Potter

Parziale points out, "Success and failure are the result of several things. I believe it's important to have a plan, a long-range plan like five years, where one can take an assessment of one's strengths and weaknesses as well as take into account the realities of one's life. For women, there is the reality of our anatomy. We have children, by choice, if we have acknowledged our control and will. There is a need for a strong support system in the home, where marriage is a partnership. I can only speak for myself, for in my life, my partnership with my husband is very important. I love sharing my success with my hus-

When it's going well, you can hardly tell one from the other; art and life are one thing.
That doesn't happen very much. And it can't be forced.
All you can do is create the conditions which allow for it.

—Louise Lamar-Fuller

Marcia Springston

Chris Dorst/The Charleston Gazette

band and I get a great deal from the companionship we share. When the children were small, I came to realize that women more than men had been socialized to set aside their own egos in order to take care of their family's needs. I longed for uninterrupted time, to sit, to think, just to rest. It was unrealistic to believe that I could be creative at the same time I was trying to raise my family. This, for me, came at a time when I had decided to be a craftsworker, and it was a time of great personal frustration. I used to brag that in my house dust was the great protector of all things, that folks would just have to get used to their sneakers sticking to the kitchen floor, and I don't believe I ever passed a test in *Cosmo*. Through enormous commitment and planning, I think my art and life are successfully combined. However, it is not easy."

This problem of combining family with work is also eloquently addressed by Lamar-Fuller. "I think it might be easier to create these conditions if you are already practicing your art before you enter relationships. That way, you have defined yourself, and the relationships are built to fit. But many women, including myself, have the relationship, the children and the obligations all in place before finding and beginning the art/work. That presents difficulties because the necessary adjustments of time and attention are apt to seem to everyone, yourself as well, to be at the expense of those you love. Doing your own work required time—and whether you take the time away from cleaning, or cooking, or earning money, or from idle TV watching evenings with your family, it costs. You have to know it's worth it, and your loved ones must be convinced of that too.

"For me, the big danger is the tendency to ricochet between demanding more help and fewer duties on the one hand and guilt and self-doubt on the other. It's tricky to find and to maintain a reasonable accommodation with those whose lives are mingled with yours; while you work on respecting and serving your own needs, you can't stop working on respecting and serving theirs. After all, being good with the people you love *is* one of your needs.

"When it's all going well, you can hardly tell one from the other; art and life are one thing. That doesn't happen very much. And it can't be forced. All you can do is try to create the conditions which allow for it."

In the Studio

Potters dream too about where and how they'd like to work, and they shared these visions. Buffy Point is insistent on the importance of good space.

"I could go on and on about an ideal work space," she says. "Lots of room, easy flow pattern, light and comfortable area, i.e., windows, good walls to put up inspiring pictures.... I have a part-time studio space downtown. Having had a studio in my home and lived with the mess of clay dust, white footprints and all the interruptions that a home work space has, makes me know I want to develop a very solid out-of-home studio. I am working on it. I feel it is easier to clear my mind and get down to work if I do not work in my home."

On the other hand, Kate Harward of Belington says, "My studio-workshop is dominated by the fact that we attached it to the house when we built it. This has meant, on the simplest level, an obsession with tracking clay through the house." But she adds it means she has never separated her art from her home and family.

Parziale and her husband work together in their studio. "Our pottery studio is divided into two work areas, each 20' x 20'. One is our space for throwing pots, the other area is for drying, glazing, and storage. We have five kilns, the largest an 80-cubic-foot downdraft flat roof car kiln. Lots of table space and an expansive open work area are essential. There can never be too many windows."

Ami Hirata has a "large 35' x 35' space with a concrete floor, great light and very well equipped with two kilns (gas and electric), ten wheels, a slab roller, a large sink, shelves, tables, a clay mixer. The duplication of equipment and size of the studio," she says, "are essential to my secondary use of the space as a teaching facility. Ideally I would like to be able to use a large gas kiln in a separate room (or out of doors), a spray booth, a large pug mill, and other mechanical aids."

Lamar-Fuller directs the Craft Shop at WVU, and has found, she says, "that the studio has shaped me as much as I have shaped it.

"Luckily, the Craft Shop has windows. The idea of working without some natural light gives me chills. Also, I think a studio should be big. A sense of expansiveness is really important. I had a painter friend who tromped on his canvases before beginning work, so they wouldn't be too precious to him. In the same vein, a potter needs *lots* of shelves, so there's no hesitation to make lots of pots. There should be lots of clay and a good system of recycling it so that using the materials doesn't seem too costly. Clay is cheap of course but if too much work is entailed in its preparation it may seem dear.

"Good results arise out of volumes of work. You need to be able to 'sketch' in clay to explore the ideas, and you need to make many pots in order to make a few good ones. If I worked in a private studio, here is where I'd spend cash: to hire someone to mix and recycle my clay, so I could feel at ease about using it freely. I'd rather spend my time making pots than making clay, just as the poet would rather make poems than the paper they're written on.

"One summer," she recalls, "I worked briefly at the Pottery Shop in Helvetia. It's a lovely little rustic building across a narrow road from the Buckhannon River, where I pulled up a big bucket of water each morning for the day's needs. There wasn't much shelving, but unless it rained, pots could be set out in the grass to dry. That quasi-outdoor work space was so delightful that the following summer I had my house wired for my kiln, and I set up a studio on the canopied terrace at home. Trees. Flowers. Deck chairs. Breezes. In my mind it was idyllic. Friends would stop by to see what I was making, to have a glass of iced tea. Up out of bed in the morning and right out to the studio with a cup of coffee.

"Then reality set in. Sounds of my working bothered the other people in the house. Condensation from the air-conditioner dropped on my wheel. Rain blew in and melted fresh pots. The kiln overfired three times before I thought to level it. Glaze splattered on the grass. And the terrace was lost to us all summer. I couldn't walk away from the work and let it rest because it was right outside the kitchen door. Now I can laugh at the disaster of it and at my naivete.

"If and when I make a studio at home again, I will separate it from our living space. I will spend money to make it right, before beginning to use it. I will think very hard about its implications. The ideal, although I may never attain it, would be to share a studio with two or three other potter friends and to have it located about two blocks from home. Working a short walk from home keeps things clear."

The Potter as Businesswoman

Business details and professional organizations are an important feature to every potter whether she likes it or not.

"There are fire potters; they are most interested in what effect they get with glazes. And there are mud potters; they concetrate on shapes," says Springston. And there are those potters who just want to make pots and wish they had a good PR man to do the selling.

"I started Wakerobin Pottery," writes Springston, "renting a two-room studio where I taught classes, produced pots and displayed and sold my works. I advertised on a local radio station and sent personal invitations announcing its opening. My business cards were handmade, with my mother cutting and stenciling the flower logo on the cover. I typed the text." She used the barter system to obtain carpentry and plumbing and furnished her showroom with antiques from a dealer. The antiques not only served to display her work, she received a commission on their sale.

"The name of our business is Sycamore Pottery," writes Parziale. "We have no plans to extend our business in the traditional sense, that is, hiring others to work for us. We like the freedom of total responsibility our pottery provides for us. If we want to experiment with salt glazing or go to another extreme, low fire earthenware, we can do so. Being creative is a balancing act between the spirit and necessity.

"My success as a craftsworker/potter is a result of not only my emphasis on good design, but is also a result of using my writing ability; my past experience in advertising and merchandising was vital in the selling of my work. Many craftworkers overlook the importance of marketing their work. It is an essential part of the total process and one that I enjoy as much as the making itself. It is important to be acknowledged as a professional in my craft just as it is important to be accepted as a business professional."

Hirata's Clayworks Studio, an unincorporated business, celebrated its opening with an open house and pottery demonstration. She belongs to no professional organizations, but occasionally does workshops, lectures, or exhibits at colleges. Mostly she works alone and likes it.

Lamar-Fuller, who has chosen to draw a dependable salary rather than put the kind of financial pressure on her work that comes from being self-employed, feels she is unusually lucky to have a job that puts her in the studio. "That doesn't mean that I get paid to do only things that I enjoy, and I still have to carve out personal time to make pots. I have noticed that each time I begin to count on money coming in from future sales, the work suffers. Without meaning to, I begin to stray away from my intentions toward my own worst renditions of marketable stuff. My pots could become very boring, to myself and everyone else, if I had to pay the rent from sales."

Springston warns that the craft business in a small Appalachian town is very vulnerable to economic forces. She, who had begun a pottery career with a small studio in her parents' garage and sold pots at crafts

Perseverance, discipline, learning—
sum them up as "craft."
Craft is the greatest resource.
It enables you to do what you
imagine. And it carries you
when your imagination
takes a vacation.

—Louise Lamar-Fuller

Pam Parziale

Parziale Pottery

fairs, found she had to move her pottery to a location with more demand in order to continue in business.

Point counts herself a novice in the market place, but has a business card and some personal advice. "The most important thing I can say about business and craft is that there is a lot of good and bad out there. Make excellent work and find your market. Good pots in the wrong setting do not sell. Where you sell, how you display and knowing the market (what people will buy, are excited about, and what they will pay) are essential."

Workshop, Gatherings, Shows

Pottery workshops, gatherings and shows are a necessity to the life of a potter. "Well, let me tell you right off that I really love hanging around other potters," exclaims Lamar-Fuller. "At big gatherings and small ones, there is so much respect, so little rivalry and envy, as to make it quite a contrast to other professional or academic groups I've seen in action. I think it's the work. No one who can be called a potter got to that point without hard sustained effort, both physical and emotional. Potters know that intimately, and it's the source of an unquestioning respect for one another as people, whether or not the pots are ones we like. Not that some individual potters aren't shmucks. But potters see an unchallengeable line of virtue in every potter.

"But most valuable, it seems to me, is the network you build for yourself, starting with other potters you know and branching out, keeping names and addresses, writing notes, doing favors, asking advice. More and more I think that the contacts you need you will get by *making* them. Speak first. Write. People are so receptive to the chance to be in touch about what matters to them."

Why Clay?

And following the path chosen brings us again to the question: What is it about this craft that attracts these artists? Why clay?

Hirata says, "My involvement is with the miraculous metamorphosis of this simple material, clay, its strength, sensuousness, color, flexibility, and resistance to unnatural force." Sprinston, who cannot see the objects that she creates, tries to achieve "a balance between tactile qualities which are important to me and the visual qualities appreciated by those who buy my work."

"I am interested in exploring form, line, and color, writes Parziale. "It is wonderful when a particularly beautiful pot comes out of the kiln. But it's always the one you never expect. It's the one that hasn't been fussed over; it's the one that is the least self-conscious. I also feel a spiritual bond to the clay. The earth is our ancestors. It will be us thousands of years from now. The earth is precious and to be treated with reverence, care and kindness. That's why I try to make beautiful pots, to express this reverence."

"If the major undertaking in life is to 'know thyself,' then clay or any serious artistic undertaking is the way to accomplish the path," Lamar-Fuller believes. "Working with clay has revealed me to myself and keeps doing so. Both the bad and the good. I've been confronted with my laziness. (That shows most visibly on the footrings and in the glazes.) I've also been surprised to recognize my own tenacity, a capacity for sustained interest and work, when I thought I was a born dilettante. I've discovered my own tastes and preference, how they came into being and continue to operate in all the artistic choices I make.

"Everything I've learned so far, and this is not a complete list, has come to me through doing—not through the play of ideas in conversation or books. I've discovered my own opinions. And I have both more humility and more respect for myself and assuredly more respect for others than I had before clay. Maybe doing anything with commitment brings the same results."

●

Resources

Berensohn, Paulus. *Finding One's Way with Clay.* New York: Simon and Schuster, 1972.

Counts, Charles. *Pottery Workshop.* New York: Macmillan, 1976.

Leach, Bernard. *A Potter's Book.* Great Britain: Transatlantic Arts Inc., 1973.

Needleman, Carla. *The Work of Craft.* Avon Books, 1981.

Nelson, Glenn C. *Ceramics: A Potter's Handbook.* New York: Holt, Rinehart and Winston, 1978.

Richard, M.C. *Centering in Pottery, Poetry, and the Person.* Wesleyan University Press, 1969.

Rhodes, Daniel. *Clay and Glazes for the Potter.* Philadelphia: Chilton Book Company, 1973.

Truitt, Anne. *Daybook: The Journal of an Artist.* Penguin, 1982.

Magazines

American Ceramics, Harry Dennis, 15 W. 44th Street, New York, New York 10036.

American Craft, American Craft Council, 401 Park Avenue South, New York, New York 10016.

Ceramics Monthly, Professional Publications, Inc., Box 12448, 1609 Northwest Blvd., Columbus, Ohio 43212.

Studio Potter, Daniel Clark Foundation, Box 65, Goffstown, New Hampshire 03045.

Supplies

Standard Ceramic Supply Co.
9 Sansbury Street
Carnegie, PA 15106
(412) 923-1655

Eagle Ceramics
12266 Wilkins Avenue
Rockville, MD 20852
(301) 881-2253

Axner Pottery
P.O. Box 1484
Oviedo, FL 32765

Barry's Office Service Inc.
1370 University Avenue
Morgantown, WV 26505

Columbus Clay Co.
1205 17th Avenue
Columbus, OH 43211

Salem Pottery Supply
179 Valley Street
Salem, WV 26426
(304) 782-1403

The Clay Place
Shadyside
Pittsburgh, PA

Crafts:

A Reflection of How We Live

Jo Silman

Carol Ann Shinn Schweiker

"I watch the hillsides change, the flowers, moss, mushrooms, all change color, and these colors seem to spill back into my baskets." These are the words of Connie McColley, who makes baskets in Chloe in Calhoun County. Like so many artists in the region who are craftworkers, McColley finds that the environment nurtures her work.

The craftworkers who shared in response to our requests are only a sampling of the fine artists who are Appalachian by choice or by chance. Their crafts are many, and they often excel at more than one. Sharing their wisdom in this section are McColley, Vivian Reynolds Pranulis, silk-screen artist of Alderson in Monroe County; Pat Burson, weaver of tapestry of Charleston in Kanawha County; Alice Stough, fiber artist of Millstone; Jan Faulkner, leather artist of Harrisburg, Pennsylvania; Melva Gillispie, maker of scrimshaw and other jewelry in Monongalia County; basketmaker Rachel Nash Law of Beverly in Randolph County; Alice Newton, quilt crafter of Harper's Ferry; Janet Hamstead, fiber artist of Charleston; Kimber Wiley, spinner/weaver, Grethe Myles, fiber artist, and Lou Ann Mohrman, maker of braided rugs, all of Morgantown; Adrienne Biesemeyer, fiber artist of Alderson; Carol Ann Shinn-Schweiker of Bristol, and Dot Montgillion, crocheter and herb crafter of Weston in Lewis County.

Some women came to their chosen craft in a pragmatic way: it was a way of making a living in their location of choice. Others discovered their medium in an epiphanic experience; almost, the art chose them.

Rachel Nash Law, a native West Virginian, first learned her art at the age of nine from her father, Charles David Nash, who had learned from watching a basketmaker at a craft fair. Law says, "My basketmaking involves the use of such materials as white oakwood, various barks such as hickory, poplar and maple, and vines and shoots. My work has its background in the tradtional basketry of the Appalachian mountains, using similar techniques and materials. I use only hand tools and nothing but winding or weaving (no nails or tacks), but an occasional wooden peg for holding the basket together."

Law has been a full-time basketmaker for eight years. Her career started with her curiosity about baskets and an interest in hand crafts of all types. But it is also an outgrowth of her childhood in a fairly self-sufficient farm family. It actually came as a shock to her that her "hobby" was both out-of-the-ordinary and marketable. "Then came the hard part," Law says, "learning about marketing and keeping books and maintaining a small production line. But before I really began producing, I was teaching basketmaking. The teaching experiences were what really made me learn my craft, having to answer those questions of why, when and how. Fortunately basketry is a very logical process and not too hard to figure out. Particularly helpful to me were Tim Pyles, Director, The

Craft Center of Ripley; Sandra Blair, Director, Arrowmont School of the Arts/Crafts in Gatlinburg, Tennessee; the Campbell Folk School, Brasstown, North Carolina; and Augusta Heritage Workshops, Elkins." Law is the author of a new book, *American White Oak Basketry: Ribs, Rods and Splits*, in collaboration with friend and colleague Cythia W. Taylor of Marietta, Ohio.

Connie McColley with her husband Tom began making baskets in the seventies. "We are children of the 60's transplanted from the city to the country in the early 70's. We live on a farm, growing our own food and living a simple lifestyle. Our baskets come from a necessity to earn a living at something while remaining on the farm. Basketry was something we tried as we searched for homesteading skills in the crafts of times past." The McColleys are self-taught. They use materials they gather locally—barks, white oak splits, honeysuckle and broomsedge. Sometimes they dye them with natural dyes, but often just blend the natural colors of the material.

"I believe our baskets are a reflection of how we live. The lines, shapes, colors are all as much a part of where we live and how we have chosen to live as they are who we are inside." Color, shape, feel and strength are important to her, whether she is working in traditional or contemporary shapes.

Vivian Pranulis became a full-time artist after years as a nurse. Yet she believes it was her childhood experiences that prepared her to be an artist. "I have always loved to draw and paint, and as a child received much encouragement from my parents. We were raised outside of Charleston in a house surrounded by large oaks, poplars, creeks and pastures.

"I never thought I would become a full-time artist. After high school, I entered the nursing program at Alderson-Broaddus College. There I met and took art classes from Herbert Waters, artist and teacher who has stayed in touch and who continues to be a source of inspiration and encouragement. I worked as an RN for a few years, but drawing and painting kept pulling me. I was able to take art classes at Kent State University, where a total re-evaluation of my life seemed to take place, and I knew I had to leave all former expectations behind. An incredible sense of freedom and creativity come with this move, and my life seemed to expand in all ways. A friend showed me the basics of silk-screen printing, and I immediately loved making these colorful prints. I met my husband, an artist and architect, and we bagan working together. Our dream was to move to the country." This they did; their home is at the end of a rural road near Alderson, a small town on the Greenbrier river.

"We continued our work with screen printing, doing prints, note cards, and calendars, and found that screen printing is endlessly challenging. We chose the name Wolf Creek Printery, and we were in business and began attending art/craft shows.

"Nature has always been an inspiration. With silk screen printing there is a wonderful element of communication. Through prints, one can share an artistic expression with many people. feel silkscreen is a real combination of art and craft. The design is created; then comes the complex craft of putting it on the screen and making prints. The art is always changed and shaped by the limits of the craft; some part of it seems to happen without conscious control."

27

Dot Montgillion's enterprise, Smoke Camp Crafts of Weston, began in retirement and grew out of her professional background. When she and her husband moved to West Virginia to "the edge of the world," as she puts it, it was appropriate that they began working with herbs, which they harvest for herb crafting. There she put her agronomy major and botany minor to use. Both she and her husband had worked for the U.S. Department of Agriculture. "What started out as a quiet retirement in 1975," she says, "has become a busy, exciting way of life."

"I began braiding rugs ten years ago," writes Lou Ann Mohrman of Morgantown, winner of a Governor's Merit Award for her work. "At that time there were few printed resources available, so the learning process was trial and error." Commitment to craft can be a lonely business, she notes. "I know of only one other person in West Virginia who makes and sells (such) rugs, so there isn't much opportunity to share ideas, problems and interests. We met several years ago and spent the week together at Ripley demonstrating rug braiding and talking rugs." However, there is a rich heritage and tradition behind rug braiding. "As I meet people at the fair it seems as though almost every other woman now in her seventies or eighties braided rugs at one time." Mohrman does business under the name *Braids*, and teaches a six-week class each fall in her home.

Janet Hamstead of Charleston ranks as perhaps one of the state's top fiber artists, yet weaving was not a lifelong passion. She first studied weaving from the well-known Lucy Quarrier through adult education programs at Garnet Center in Charleston, and only about five years ago turned part-time professional. Now she weaves mainly clothing: beautiful classic tops, skirts, dresses and shawls, marketing them through Studio 40 at the Greenbriar, the WV Artists and Craftmens Guild Gallery in Charleston, and Artwear in Chicago. "In my woven clothing at this time, I am trying to concentrate on the interplay of color, line and texture. Although classic, simple lines allow the fabric to be seen, the human form must also be taken into consideration. What I am striving for is clothing that not only enhançes the person but becomes part of the human spirit."

The Craftswoman at Work

"Your art is your life."

—*Pat Burson*

Hamstead and her husband Bob, a CPA who advises her bookkeeping, have indeed become a "weaver's family." She converted their living room into a studio which holds three looms built by a husband she describes as "very supportive." The dining room is used as a sewing room when needed.

Hamstead relies on the Craft Center at Cedar Lakes for her continuing education. There she has taken courses in ikat weaving, color theory, off-loom weaving, spinning, pattern drafting, fabric design, and photography. Her first teaching experience was also at the Craft Center. She recommends the West Virginia Artists and Craftmens Guild for learning product improvement.

Pat Burson, weaver of tapestry, knows colors. In fact, she may use as many as 400 colors in one tapestry. Tapestry is a commissioned art, and thus, Burson says, it is a collaborative effort, reflecting not only her personality but that of the person or persons for whom it is being produced.

Early in the design process, Burson chooses a palette of color which to a great extent will determine the mood or tone of the woven piece. Inspiration often comes from the world of nature—wilderness and sunlight after a storm and the beach. Or it may come from the work of John Singer Sargent, Picasso, Mozart, Delacroix, O'Keeffe, or Rubens. Both the design and the size of the tapestry are of course influenced by the needs of the client, the space, and the money available. Both client and artist approve the design before the weaving begins, which will take from three to six months. The completed design is then enlarged photographically to the actual size of the tapestry.

Burson then dresses her twelve-foot loom with linen warp threads, and weaves with the finest wool yarns avilable, spun and dyed in Sweden. With two assistants, she works at eye level, bulding the fabric and watching the design grow in fractions of inches. As it is woven, the fabric is rolled onto a beam near the bottom of the loom. Like a good carpet, the tapestry will be finished by stretching, blocking, and the attachment of a sturdy backing. At last it is prepared for hanging.

Burson's work space is a separate section set apart from the home, very tightly organized. Another room is used for office area and drawing room. The living room is her weaving room. Pat believes it is important to use the best equipment money can buy, and to keep a good inventory. A good filing system, bookkeeping system, and cross references to the filing system are necessities. She would prefer an office/studio that is separate from her home.

Another fiber artist, Alice Stough of Millstone, who operates Alice in Wonderland Creations, truly begins at the source. "We breed our sheep for color, and now have a flock of about 50 shades of black, brown and gray. My husband grows organic food for the sheep and does all the shearing. I wash the fleece I'm going to use, and handcard and spin the wool into yarn, then knit sweaters, hats, scarves, ponchos, and blankets."

Kimber Wiley, a spinner and weaver who calls her business "Nature's Own," works "in a happy area filled with plants, birds, and sunlight, a place almost like being outdoors." She uses wool from area farms (she recommends the county extension office for information), also animal fibers from dogs and goats. She keeps angora rabbits and spins directly from their hair.

Adrienne Biesemeyer of Alderson uses her initials in AB *Textiles Design*. She also belongs to *Group Cottage Hill Designers*. Her workspace is in her home—a 20' by 18' studio with an 18-foot counter and 12-foot wall bins for yarn. Her two children, one a pre-schooler, often play or do art work in the studio with her.

When other couples were buying furnishings and shopping for a home," writes jewelry designer Jane Campbell of Cambridge Springs, Pennsylvania, "we were buying machinery and looking for a studio space (my husband Bill is a potter). We found a large empty ivy-covered building that had been a steam plant for one of the big resort hotels back when taking the waters was popular.

"When I got out of college and started making jewelry I found a hole in the market; no one was making brass and copper finished as perfectly as gold. Any brass and copper you saw was hobby type hammer-marked stuff." Campbell shares an office and office manager with her husband, and they "work all the income and expenses out

Linda McKay Young

Nancy Abrams

of one set of books. That way if one of us is selling better or worse, the other can carry through a dry month. Our business is prospering mostly because of the immense time and energy we put into it; we are always working. We work evenings and weekends year round. We have no children and find the production and selling of our artwork so fascinating that it is like entertainment to us. I can't imagine anything else."

Campbell says, "We market our work under our own names so that a customer realizes that there is a real person behind it. Many purist craftspeople are against having a staff, but I enjoy it. I have four carefully picked women that I have taught to make things exactly as I do, and they keep me company. We are all surviving together financially. Some of them have children so they work irregular hours; others have their own creative ambitions and are with me until they get their own art going. We are helping each other."

Another craft team are the Gillispies, Melva and Joe, who together run the Horn and Antler Shop in Morgantown, which specializes in scrimshaw, as well as jewelry in many forms. "Fulfillment in one's craft results from perseverance and determination," writes Melva Gillispie. "Patience is the requirement for scrimshaw."

Veteran of ten years in the professional craft field, Gillispie finds that fulltime craft requires that "someone else be footing the living expenses." The Gillispies silkscreen wildlife tee-shirts for much of their steady income, but that isn't what they particularly want to do. "Working is so wonderful if you can choose what you really enjoy, but making a living isn't always a pleasure."

She finds herself constantly attending workshops and studying both books and nature. "I'm still learning, and new ideas require addtional training." A continuing interest in one's craft, she believes, comes from curiosity about new developments.

Dot Montgillion and her husband Bob operate Smoke Camp Crafts from their farm on Smoke Camp Run in Lewis County, which borders on a game preserve. There they harvest traditional Appalachian herbs for herb crafting and berries for their unusual jellies and jams. Dot Montgillion creates original designs in crochet and writes about herbs. "I have a 20 by 24 foot workshop for jam/jelly and herb preparation next to home. The workshop has an enclosed porch for storage with a drying room. These were built to my specifications, so it's pretty much what I need except could always use more storage space. All yarns are kept in a spare room in the house." They built their workshop and gift outlet with the help of a good friend. Its main heat sources are two solar heat grabbers.

Montgillion's book, *Modern Uses of Traditional Herbs*, is available from Smoke Camp Crafts by mail. She enjoys people's delighted reactions at seeing some of her traditional herbs and jellies. "I haven't seen that jam (or that herb) since my grandma fixed it!" She even supplies a local doctor with several herbs which he has used successfully in his practice.

Rachel Nash Law describes her working situation as a work room that can be closed off from the rest of the house, with a work bench and lots of light from large windows, and an overhead bench light. "These are the essentials. The rest is secondary. The self discipline of working at home is always a battle, particularly when the work is not very interesting."

The Craftswoman as Teacher

Many craftswomen spoke of the importance of teaching in their lives as artists. Basketmaker Law, who had to turn down teaching in order to write her book, found that she missed it immensely. "The contact with people and the opportunity to see what is current are the two most inspirational factors for my work."

Alice Newton, quiltmaker (see the chapter on quilts), who operates a quilting business "Patches" in Harper's Ferry, affirms the value of teaching. "For me teaching others is what helps keep me growing and changing. Eyes, new and innocently looking at techniques I'm using, lead me to new insights."

Montgillion has found her knowledge of herb lore has an outlet in teaching. She counts it as a milestone when she gave lectures on herbal medicine at the Herbal Medicine Symposium of 1985 at Marshall University Medical School.

Lifestyle Choices

Grethe Myles of Morgantown is a public school teacher. This means that she can afford the luxury of pleasing herself in her work as a fiber artist. During her term as president of the West Virginia Art Education Association, she virtually gave up the making of art, but intends to work again with wearables. "My wearables are made for my own pleasure and for gifts." Myles, with no children, says she is "married to a co-workaholic. We share household chores equally and both love to cook. (Whoever cooks is exempt from cleanup.) It's important to have a spouse who understands and is supportive of one's creative endeavors."

Myles is "blessed with a large room to work in. I have a desk (used for sewing, which belonged to my grandfather), a drafting table, double file, large hutch, two closets, storage bins. Wish I had a skylight but feel fortunate with what have."

Dick Pranulis

Vivian Pranulis

McColley's work space is small. "I work at the kitchen table," she says. "My children ages five and six play at my feet or sit beside me and do 'school.' I take the major responsibility for their schooling. However, the children know that when I have a show or deadline, I just work and can't give them as much time. I work mostly after dinner until midnight.

"I must have order in my space, and I need to arrange and straighten it once a day before I can begin work. It doesn't stay that way long, but this fills that need in me. Ideally, would like more space separate from my living area." She and her husband share the cooking and household chores. Since they work together at their craft, they find such sharing is essential for successful living.

Mohrman says she has discovered the joys of an empty nest. "I didn't start braiding until all the children were in school. As they have grown and moved out, I've moved into empty bedrooms and now am using one for wool storage, one for other supplies, and the rest of the house for a work room. As the size of the rug progresses, I move from one area to another. I have a commercial machine that I use to stitch my wool strips together."

Hamstead has given her priorities a great deal of thought. At this point in her career, she says, family comes first, then weaving, then home. "At times the order is reversed, but only for short periods. I have done and continue to do all child care, cooking, and housework." Now that her children are older (fourteen and eight), she finds she can spend from 8:30 am to 2:15 pm each day on weaving. "Evenings, I work in our family room with my family." For her, the key word is "choice." "Each person has to find her own priorities and ways to deal with them. It is OK that I write 'homemaker' on application forms instead of 'weaver.' Some people have to have that job title."

The Philosophy of a Craftswoman

"I love people," explains leather artist Jan Faulkner of Harrisburg, Pennsylvania. "Creating beautiful garments to adorn the human form is a perfect means for me to express that. prefer creating one-of-a-kind pieces, because these relate to the uniqueness of each one of us." Faulkner has been both designing and teaching in the field of applied decoration for leather garments since 1972. Despite her enthusiasm, there is also ambivalence. "Doing clothing as a medium for creative expression has been a double-edged sword. I love that connection when it makes people feel good about themselves when they wear my piece. But I struggle sometimes accepting myself as an artist, and not just a fashion designer which, though creative, is not serious enough for me. Then at those times I reach into myself and bring out a piece like my "FAN Kimono" to prove myself.

"Being creative has given me not only a way to earn a living but a life that gives me room, freedom. My work is also my play. It's fun and there are times I laugh about how I will never grow up now because I am forever playing—going from doll clothes as a kid to larger doll clothes as an adult—I love it!"

Pat Burson describes combining art and life thus: "Your art is your life. It has to be as fully integrated as possible. Some can manage a nine-to-five operation, turn it off and on, and I truly admire those people. Unless you have a burning desire to become an artist and have

If anyone wonders why on earth a woman, single parent of three, below poverty level income, part-time instructor of art in a small liberal arts college, West Virginia native, age 46 (they never include me in polls— I meet all the criteria of the disadvantaged) should be seriously painting and showing those paintings, trying to get accepted in a degree program, just beginning the craft show circuit, doing creative writing, and starting a small "in-home" arts crafts studio— it's because somewhere I heard that many female artists of previous and immediate generations didn't begin their greatest creative spurt until mid-life, usually thought of as the myopic, migrainous and menopausal decades.

—Carol Ann Shinn Schweiker

a tremendous amount of self-descipline, I wouldn't bother. I'd just get a nine-to-five job like the rest of the world. Make it easy on yourself." Burson has her children watched by someone in a private home. Of course, she says, "It's much easier when kids are in school. There are times when I can work with them. At ages five and seven my sons are able to help somewhat to wind the yearns and arrange the color table, and even do a little bit of weaving and drawings. At meal times—thank goodness for peanut butter and jelly and Wendy's and a husband who out of desperation is going to learn to cook. When the dust gets too thick, I hire a professional."

Alice Newton shares her solution for a slump in creativity. "I rationalize that everyone should get at least two weeks' paid vacation a year, and I have a reading binge, six or seven books a week. If I'm still not on track, then I give myself a second week." When this time is up, she says, "I make myself sit down and start to work on the production stuff we all have to do to survive—the thing we sometimes hate to do. Make yourself do it and soon—very soon—you are back on your creative base again. Don't forget, this whole process is an inner struggle and not one easily won."

The Craftswoman as Businesswoman

Getting one's work to the public is central to the growth of both artist and person, believes Newton. She sees it as an evolutionary process with distinct stages: a) excitement that someone wants what I have to sell, b) "I've got to see who I'm selling to," c) acceptance or rejection—I am on the line, not what I am selling, d) drawing back from direct sale/consumer contact, e) reaffirming of self as artist but dealing with middleman/wholesaler, f) clinical manufacture of a product to which I am no longer tied. Some people never progress beyond the first tow. That's O.K. Those who hit "f" are ready to work for IBM instead of themselves.

For Law, timing and location have been crucial to her professional development as a craftswoman. She first began when the region was undergoing a revival of traditional crafts, and the state was actively encouraging this. The continued interest in country decoration as well as the popularity of basketry both as craft and as collection have helped. Law markets her work through word of mouth, mail order, several steady shop and gallery accounts, and craft fairs.

She has no intention of expanding her business. "This is definitely a one-person operation and I intend to stay that way." She uses only her own name for her business and is not incorporated. An accountant takes care of the books. Her advice to someone just starting out is to "learn as much as possible about your craft, be the best craftsperson possible, and then 'hit the road' to show your product through juried exhibitions, fairs, shows, etc."

Carol Ann Shinn-Schweiker, artist, teacher, and craftswoman of Bristol, has some advice for beginners having their work reviewed by juries, shops and catalogue outlets. Such reviewers accept nothing assembled from commercially-sold kits, and their criteria generally include these: 1) quality of craftsmanship and thoroughness of finishing, 2) general excellence of concept, design, and execution, and 3) sensitivity in the use of the medium.

Mohrman does most of her rugs as commissioned orders, marketing some through semi-annual shows in Morgantown, in Charleston through the Cultural Center where slides of her rugs are available, and through the *Goodfellow Catalog of Wonderful Things* (1981), a constant source of inquiry. "My problem is not finding markets, but production. Rug braiding is extremely labor intensive, and I've never found anyone who would like to help with the production." A second problem, she notes, is tendonitis, a problem common to spinners and potters as well. "Our retirement plan (had) included locating in some area with a high interest in crafts where I would braid the rest of my life; that doesn't seem likely now."

*Design is the key
to whatever you do
in any medium.*
—Diane Bosley

Two of Montgillion's suggestions are, "Send public relations material to newspapers in the area of craft shows you will be attending— the advertising is free!" and "If your craft fits, try museum shops." Also, "Join your regional travel council. They promote members and distribute your brochures." Montgillion, together with the Lewis County members of the WV Artists and Craftsmens Guild, solved a marketing problem in their rural county. The civic-minded owner of a hardware store in Weston allows the group to display their crafts on the mezzanine of the spacious store. The association has proved beneficial to both sides. One of the members, Leslie Mulliken, has set up a yarn shop and studio at one end, and thus is available to handle craft sales for the others. This, Montgillion says, has proved ideal for the group which could otherwise not afford to rent a building.

Smoke Camp Crafts is not incorporated, she says, but would be if she had employees or if she was starting out at an early age. People recognize her logo, which she uses on labels, business cards, stationery, gift boxes, and table covers used at shows. "Expansion comes with experience. Like life in general, as one progresses values and goals refocus and change. Can't expect to make a million the first year. Crawl before you walk. As your skill increases, your creativity will expand."

McColley says emphatically, "The business work is as important as the work itself." Most people have found out about them by word of mouth and seeing the 'hang tags' on baskets sold. "Expansion makes me think of other ways to use my craft to generate income, not only wholesale, retail, mail order and commission, but also teaching and lecturing. Now we are making baskets which are large outdoor sculptures and we wonder where this could go. We are anxious to see, as we look for an event to apply these new ideas. I think you must re-examine what you are doing and where you want to go with your work all the time."

Quilting: A Sense of Wholeness

Cheryl Torsney

"What is a quilt?" asks Miriam Schapiro in her essay "Geometry and Flowers" (Charlotte Robinson's *The Artist and the Quilt*). Her response indicates the importance quilting, as both pastime and art, has had for generations of women across the country: "Among other things, it is the history of women, a receptacle of passions, attitudes, largesse, and anger. It is a reassembling process, which in itself may embody a solution to human problems. It is inspiration, a connection with self, the dogged will to make something extraordinary in the midst of family routine, a sense of wholeness, the wish to please, to succeed, pleasure in the act of working and knowing the power of 'making.'"

Many West Virginia quilters, in their passion for the craft, have discovered their own histories and have reattached themselves to their roots. Having learned quilting from mothers, grandmothers, aunts, and cousins, some think of it as a private activity carried on within the boundaries of family space. Nancy Klein, a quilting instructor in Morgantown, first became interested in quilting after observing two elderly women pass time quilting during a lonely time in their lives and a lonely time in her life. A retired university professor says that she associates quilts with her youth: "When my father read aloud— my grandmother, mother, sister and I quilted." Seventy-five-year-old Ada Belle Cottrell of Spencer learned quilting from her maternal grandmother; all of the women in her family quilt. Her favorite quilt she created as a gift for her daughter out of scraps of white, lilac, and violet satin and brocade from her daughter's wedding gown and her bridesmaids' gowns. Cottrell's goal is to give quilts to all of her grand and great-grandchildren before her arthritis gets the best of her.

Although they do not put it in quite these terms, quilting women in West Virginia would probably find themselves exemplifying Lucy R. Lippard's observation that "Since the new wave of feminist art began around 1970, the quilt has become the prime metaphor for women's lives, for women's culture" (in Robinson's *The Artist and the Quilt*).

Quilting serves to connect quilters quite privately, not only with their personal pasts but also to a larger group of women with similar interests. Like the quilting bees of the past, today's quilting guilds and organizations serve as a social outlet for their members. While quilting and the bees formerly marked passages in the lives of girls and women, meetings of quilting organizations in recent years offer similar opportunities for socializing—and perhaps even, as in the past, for political consciousnesss raising. Susan B. Anthony gave her first talk on the issue of equal rights for women at a quilting bee. Klein observes: "The socializing benefits of our modern guild must be comparable to early quilting bees. A modern quilting bee provides the same personal, social, political and religious outlet our grandmothers experienced!"

Like earlier groups, today's quilting clubs boast a varied membership. As Carter Houck observes of the Blue Ridge Quilters, "The quilters we met in our two days at Harper's Ferry were a marvelously varied group, old, young, enterprising business women, wives of Washington commuters, but quilt enthusiasts one and all. There were women whose mothers and grandmothers had quilted and women who had only begun to learn about quilting a year or two ago. The feeling of energy and excitement was, as seems always to be the case with quilters, completely contagious" ("The Blue Ridge Quilters" in *Lady's Circle Patchwork Quilts*).

Indeed, the same is true of two quilting groups in Morgantown, the Campus Quilting Interest Group and the Country Roads Quilting Guild. Among the members of these groups are a hairdresser, a manager, a library director, several teachers, a retired professor, an assistant professor of computer science, a former police officer, the assistant director of the West Virginia University MBA program, a secretary, a physical therapist, a medical technologist, and several homemakers and housewives. Their ages and quilting experience also vary widely their ages from 30 to 71, their experience from six months to sixty years. The Country Roads Quilting Guild is a typical group. Organized three years ago, it now has 35 members. Its purpose, as stated in the publicity released before its most recent show, "is to encourage an interest in quilting through learning and sharing, widen the circle of friends with a common interest, and improve creativity and skills." Nearly all of them express the feeling that quilting stitches an energy and enthusiasm through the fabric of their lives.

Although it may seem contradictory, despite the energy, productivity, excitement, even obsession, associated with the process of quilting, the piecing and quilting of fabric seems to offer each quilter a sense of peace and calm, a noiseless room of her own. Sometimes, however, it is difficult to get from the hallway into that room. Alice Newton of Bakerton, co-owner of the quilting supply shop Patches, Inc., explains: "It is very difficult for others to understand you are working when you don't leave the house and when you are doing something you so thoroughly enjoy." Schapiro has described that feeling of calm as "discovering that making something beautiful heals exhaustion; it is finding what it is to be next to the stars." Or, as a quilter incarcerated in the Mississippi State Penitentiary on a murder charge explains about quilting, "It gives me constellation." Little did she know that in her slip of the tongue, she reached deeply into the reasons many women quilt. The sense of the quilter is that her craft pieces together bits of time frequently stolen from other tasks. Morgantown quilter Kris Potter writes, "I like to know that I can spend two hours with a needle, thread and fabrics and have an end result—complete or not—as opposed to two hours of cleaning house that is messed/dirtied the next day." Quilting soothes Potter and many other quilters, putting them at peace with themselves and the world.

The creative potential inherent in the crafting of quilts intrigues many quilters—piecers, quilt artists, and poets who treat the quilt thematically and metaphorically—more than the social or psychological potential of quilting. In her poem "Looking at Quilts," Marge Piercy

"Quilting . . . offers each quilter a sense of peace and calm, a noiseless room of her own."

"It is very difficult for others to understand you are working when you don't leave the house and when you are doing something you thoroughly enjoy."

—Alice Newton

writes about quilting as a metaphor for the revitalizing quality of creativity:

> the quilt might be
> the only perfect artifact a woman
> would ever see, yet she did not doubt
> what we had forgotten, that out of her
> potatoes and colic, sawdust and blood
> she could create; together, alone
> she seized her time and made new.

Her sentiment seems to echo an anonymous voice from an earlier time: "Sometimes you don't have no control over the way things are. Hail ruins the crops, or fire burns you out and then you're just given so much to work with in a life and you have to do the best you can with what you got. That's what piecing is. The materials is passed on to you, or is all you can afford. But the way you put them together is your business. You can put them in any order you like."

Like all quilters, West Virginians who engage in the art delight in the creative freedom quilting offers. Bob Douglas, a quilt artist who lives on a a farm ouside Berkeley Springs, speaks of an 1870's crazy quilt from which she drew inspiration. "It was my grandmother's. I borrowed a stitch from it to use on Ruffled Waters [a figure in an art quilt she collaborated on with Harmony Hammond]. The stitch is very Victorian and ornate. I love this quilt now that I've finished. When I first started, I hated the thought of all that quilting, but all those days spent hunched over the quilting frame have really paid off. All the textures in the quilt have made it richer and richer—like a tapestry."

Thirty-four-year-old housewife Theda Sanders writes that quilting is her "main creative outlet," that quilting keeps her sane while she is "stuck at home with young children." Although she will look at books for ideas, she rarely follows instructions, working independently. "It makes me think and create in a personal way," Sanders states.

"I view it as my special craft—a way to express myself artistically—a way to share with other women too," comments Maureen Busche-Terman. Suzanne Gainer, a medical technologist, agrees that quilting "serves as a form of artistic expression." She writes of an experience that brought that feeling home to her: "As an assignment for a group I once participated in, I was to take a picture that was representative of me to share with the group. I chose a picture of crazy quilt. The pieces seemed to stand for the many parts or roles in my life—daughter, wife, mother, friend, student, searcher, etc. Each little patch is different, but the total piecing effect makes me. I sometimes wonder what patch I will add to the quilt called ME next." Teacher Jeanne Gren expresses what she views as the double-sided creative quality of quilting. When she makes her bed, she explains, "I feel more than proud—it's as if the love that went into making it and the love that goes on under it combine to make even more."

Many discover their creative spirits in revising traditional patterns. Favorites include the Schoolhouse, the Dresden Plate ("It reminds me of a Dutch china pattern I own," comments Susan Farmer, a student records assistant in Morgantown), the Wedding Ring and Double Wedding Ring, the Log Cabin, and the Flower Garden ("It's one of the first quilts I remember," writes Morgantown housewife Elaine Hutchinson). Many quilters agree that choosing a preferred pattern is impossible since they love so many. Potter admits honestly that her favorite pattern is whichever one she's working on. And only till she's *halfway* through piecing the quilt.

In *The Southern Review* (Summer 1985) Houston A. Baker, Jr., and Carlotte Pierce-Baker have explained: "A patch is a fragment. It is a vestige of a wholeness that stands as a sign of loss and a challenge to creative design. As a remainder or remnant, the patch may symbolize rupture and impoverishment; it may be defined by the faded glory of the already gone. But as a fragment or remnant, it is also rife with explosive potential of the yet-to-be-discovered. Like a woman, it is a liminal element between wholes." Like the patches of the symbolic quilt described by Baker and Pierce-Baker, the quilting women of West Virginia are also "rife with explosive potential of the yet-to-be-discovered." They are enthusiastically pursuing a hobby and a tradition that both link them to the past and promise them a fruitful future. As Cindy Jopling of Morgantown asserts, "It's contagious—being around quilters and sharing ideas is motivating and stimulating."

●

Resources

Books

Bishop, Robert, et al. *Quilts, Coverlets, Rugs & Samplers.* New York: Alfred A. Knopf, 1982.

Colby, Averil. *Quilting.* New York: Scribner, 1972.

Hall, Carrie A. and Kretsinger, Rose G. *The Romance of the Patchwork Quilt in America.* New York: Bonanza Books, 1935.

Hopkins, Mary Ellen. *The It's OK If You Sit on My Quilt Book.* Atlanta, GA: Yours Truly, 1982.

Houck, Carter. *The Patchwork Pattern Book.* New York: Dutton, 1981.

Ickis, Margaret. *The Standard Book of Quilt Making and Collecting.* New York: Dover Publications, 1959.

James, Michael. *The Quiltmaker's Handbook: A Guide to Design and Construction.* Englewood Cliffs, NJ: Prentice-Hall, 1978.

——————————————. *The Second Quiltmaker's Handbook: Creative Approaches to Contemporary Quilt Design.* Englewood Cliffs, NJ, 1981.

King, Elizabeth. *Quilting.* New York: Leisure League of America, 1984.

Leone, Diane. *The Sampler Quilt,* 6th ed. Santa Clara, CA: Leone Publication, 1985.

Lipsett, Linda Otto. *Remember Me: Women and Their Friendship Quilts.* San Francisco, CA: The Quilt Digest Press, 1985.

Lithgow, Marilyn. *Quiltmaking and Quiltmakers.* New York; Funk and Wagnalls, 1974.

Mahler, Celine Blanchard. *Once Upon a Quilt: Patchwork Design and Technique.* New York: Van Nostrand Reinhold, 1973.

Irwin, John Rice. *A People and Their Quilts.* Exton, PA: Schiffer Publication, 1983. (on Appalachian quilting)

Ramsey, Dan and Beyer, Jinny. *Patchwork Patterns.* McLean, VA: EPM Publications, 1979.

————————————————. *The Quilter's Album of Blocks and Borders.* McLean, VA: EPM Publications, 1980.

Robinson, Charlotte, ed. *The Artist and the Quilt.* New York; Alfred A. Knopf, 1983.

Articles

Mainardi, Patricia. "Quilts, the Great American Art." *The Feminist Art Journal* 2 (1): 1, 18-23.

Miller, Lynn F. and Swenson, Sally S. *Lives and Works: Talks with Women Artists.* (interview with quilter Radka Donnell-Vogt.) Metuchen, NJ: Scarecrow Press, 1981.

Magazines

Decorating and Craft Ideas
Lady's Circle Patchwork Quilts
Needlecraft for Today
The New American Quilt
Quilt
Quilter's Newsletter Magazine
Work Basket

Films

"Quilting Women," Appalshop Films. 27 minutes, color, sound, 16 mm.

"Quilts in Women's Lives." New Day Films. 28 minutes, color, sound, 16 mm.

Organizations

Cabin Creek Quilts, Cabin Creek, WV 25035.

Country Roads Quilt Guild, c/o Suzanne Gainer, 156 Poplar Dr., Morgantown, WV 26505.

Mountain Heritage Quilters Guild, 605 E. Park, Apt. 2, Fairmont, WV 26554.

Patches, Inc., 1499 Washington St., Rt. 3, Box 66, Harpers Ferry, WV 25425 (Pat Kidwilder and Alice Newton, owners).

Miscellaneous

Katy and David Fidler, P.O. Box 80, Harpers Ferry, WV 25425. They silk-screen beautiful prints of quilt designs.
Quilt Digest Press, Dept. D, 955 Fourteenth St., San Francisco, CA 94114. The press offers a wide range of books on quilting.

Stained Glass: Not a Forgiving Craft

Mary Lynn Ganahl

There is magic in glass. Viewing one of the great rose windows of European cathedrals, it is hard to believe that the main component is earth's most ancient and simple of inorganic substances — silica sand. But with the addition of ash (for strength), minerals or oxides (for color), and the heat associated with the world's birth, these ingredients become glass, a substance that makes light dance. Adding light adds life. A stained glass creation has its own life for it changes with light — with the day, with the season, with the weather.

As a glass craftswoman I am always brought back to my worktable by the glass — the fun of playing with the colors and textures of glass, each piece interpreting light in its own way as we interpret our lives in ways unique to ourselves.

West Virginia artists have been drawn to the craft in various ways. Meg Barton of Chloe found it a natural move to stained glass from a background in painting. "I am a painter at heart, and doing stained glass is like painting with color or painting with light. It comes alive." Ann Contois' background led her to a career in glass. As a child in Europe the Hamlin artist sat for long periods of time in churches. She escaped the boredom of sermons in a foreign tongue, she says, "by delighting in watching the light change, the alive, magic and fascinating images floating in the stone traceries above our heads."

For an artist, glass affords special opportunities and new dimensions for creativity, because the glass is never static. A window may be the artist's creation, but it is transformed as soon as it is held up for the sun to enliven. Contois says, "I feel I have always been enthralled by glass, the moods it can create with color and line and form, the catalytic effect it seems to have on the imagination, surrounding you with light to both affect the environment you are in, and at the same time draw you to itself." Not only transformed as light passes through it, glass passes on that transformation to its surroundings as the colors reflect in rooms. Passive only in the absence of light, glass draws a viewer's interest, and the creativity of the artist passing through the creation inspires the viewer.

It is the potential for inspiration that so stirs Contois' imagination. "This is the creation there has never been," she quotes from the poet Rilke. "I am particularly interested in this aspect of firing of the imagination, as I feel fantasy and illusion are such fragile concepts in our practical high-tech society.

Design and Recreation

In stained glass there are potentially two phases of creativity. The original moment is the designing of the piece: the artist's idea merging with colors, textures, lines, and forms. Translating the quality of the idea into a blueprint (cartoon) becomes the measure of the finished product as a work of art. Diane Bosley of Mineral Wells says quite simply, "Design is the key to whatever you do in any medium."

The second creative phase is completely dependent on the success of the first, for if successfully rendered, the artist's fantasy-made design is preserved and re-created time and again as the viewer's imagination is fired.

Between these two phases is a period when artist is craftsperson, concentrating on making the design a finished piece. Stained glass is not a forgiving craft; it allows no shortcuts, no room for sloppiness. Mistakes leave a messy edge or a shattered piece of glass destined for the trash. There is little room for adjustment or compensation. When cutting and soldering glass, I work best in a state of detached concentration. Alert and attentive to what I am doing, part of me needs to be completely relaxed and at peace with what I am doing. Pressure on the small wheel that scores the glass must come evenly from my shoulder through my arm, not just from my hand, as if I were cutting the glass with energy flowing from my center. After spending a long time with a particularly difficult piece only to have it break in a final trim, the art demands that I throw it away and start again, concentrating on the process, not the product. If upset, I will just break more. There is personal growth I can measure in myself through this 'detachment' as I cut, foil, and solder — maturity that means less ego is invested in outer things, and more maintained calmly inside myself.

The Business of Glass

It is fortunate that working with glass is so fulfilling, for like quilting, it is impossible to sell a finished piece for its true worth. Materials (glass, solder, copper foil, and lead) are expensive and may be as much as 20-50% of the selling cost. And the time investment is very high. For these reasons, there are few stained glass artists in West Virginia living entirely from a stained glass income. Most artists work in other fields, either full- or part-time, and while this employment takes valuable time away from artistic work, it eases the pressure to produce marketable pieces.

Bosley, with a full-time job, has complete freedom in glass work, though limited time. "My present work is for self-fulfillment and personal growth. I do one-of-a-kind pieces that excite and stimulate me. I decided to let go of the craft fairs that are for the $20 market item and look for gallery exhibits and commissions that allow complete expression of myself."

Denise Hight of St. Albans is "finding it very tough to make a good living in crafts, at least in West Virginia. I'm originally from Washington, DC. It's probably easier in a large metro area. Business growth is higher there. Our unemployment is still very high, so people don't have a lot of money to spend. So, to be honest, anyone who wants to get into crafts full-time should be prepared for some lean times. Or he/she might want to get a part-time job for awhile until it's known if the craft could support him/her.

Barton, a part-time graphics designer, echoes this: "I really don't believe I could do it full-time and make a living. Crafts are wonderful, but I don't know any rich craftspeople. I don't believe they exist, at least not in West Virginia."

The few committed to stained glass full-time face a difficult challenge, requiring resourcefulness and deep faith in one's talents.

"Stained glass is my sole source of livelihood — it is **very** difficult to do in West Virginia," says Contois. Most of her sales come from out of state or through commissions, shops and shows. Teaching the craft augments her income, but she does it "mainly to increase layman appreciation and create an educated buying public."

Nyoka Baker, an independent glass artist in Huntington, is dependent on commissions, sales, and prizes. She also teaches classes, but does no fairs or craft shows. "I don't invest in making speculative works that are not what I consider art, i.e., I don't create commercial pieces for sale. As a profession, I could only recommend it to those who are serious about their work. Self-employment in any field is always a gamble. One must have confidence in himself/herself and the work and be tenacious and extremely hardworking."

Selling the work is the bottom line for the artist trying to be self-supporting. Commissions are the best, especially when there is freedom to create, but these are hard to get. Craft shows and fairs provide outlets for some kinds of work, but Baker points out that high-priced works find little or no market at fairs. However, Bosley discovered displaying work at one festival each year encourages local commissions.

Selling through shops is an alternative, though they may keep as much as 30-50% of a selling price, leaving little profit given the high cost of materials. But this frees the artist's time, and a reasonable arrangement gives valuable exposure. A work hanging in a shop can lead to further orders and commissions.

Ann Contois and Denny Hight have displayed work at Glass Act, a five-member stained glass cooperative in Charleston. The advantages of a group arrangement are tremendous as members share time in the store, leaving time free to work. Cooperatives make it possible for artists to afford a more prestigious location, and the variety of styles of work draws a larger buying public.

Shows can be the best way to reach a large, educated market, particularly for larger, more expensive pieces. Some are difficult to enter as they are selective about the work allowed and often are juried, but the quality of the works gives these shows a status seldom afforded the fairs. The Appalachian Glass Society has a show once or twice yearly, and the Cultural Center in Charleston has one very selective show annually. The Cultural Center also places works in shops at the state parks.

Women choosing stained glass for a career, either full- or part-time, chose a medium both fulfilling and endlessly fascinating. Its demands seem minor when one is creating, but taken seriously, the art leaves little space for life away from it. Hight finds such conflicts are difficult. "A lot of us work between 10-12 hours per day or more than 70 hours per week. If you're married with children it's got to be impossible to do. I'm married with no children, and it's impossible. Sometimes those you live with feel you're not paying enough attention to them, or they resent having to help out a little more. Then there is that time of night when they are ready to go to sleep and your head is spinning with all sorts of thoughts and you're not sleepy. It can and will create problems. When your show is around the corner, you have to pack up and leave home for maybe a week or a weekend. You just have to talk a lot of things out and hope it works. So far for me it has . . . every one of my friends in stained glass, I think, has had to deal with it."

Relationships with fellow artists may be the best and easiest of your relationships or the most difficult to make work. While lifestyles may blend, two egos in need of nurturing may not. Bosley and husband Norm Sartorius have the best of both worlds, she believes. "I met my husband at the Mountain State Arts and Crafts Fair. We have a wonderful working and loving relationship and share all the responsibilities of the household. He is the main cook and I do the majority of the cleaning. He is a full-time woodworker-sculptor, and my experiences with him have opened new doors to a world I didn't realize existed. We help each other and realize each other's needs, which include time together and time alone."

As with any creative medium, the key to growth as a stained glass artist is growth as a person. But there are concrete things one can do to develop and perfect the craft. Bosley took watercolor and drawing lessons and feels "there are major limitations without these tools. I often had a wonderful idea but was unable to transfer it to paper." Other classes helped less directly but in equally important ways. "I have taken classes in breath, voice, and movement and find it is all part of the whole which helps creativity to flow."

Reflecting on an accident which seriously injured her husband and kept her away from stained glass for seven months, Bosley realizes that her life changed. "During the early time of the accident, the surgeries, the fact that life for us together was so close to being cut off brought forth a deeper look at the spiritual side." The work became a mirror of life, a way to step back and see, perhaps understand.

"There have been various times when there were many pieces to pick up, but each time new strength came and new boundaries were crossed. All of this makes up me, the way I see the world and the way I try to express it." Planning a pattern to be transformed by suffusion of light, the glass artist defines, shares, re-experiences, and finally understands her life. Bosley speaks for all artists. "I am looking forward to getting back to glass and seeing the effects of this experience and the changes it will bring in my art."

Getting Started in West Virginia

In sources below offer classes taught by some of the best artists in the region. However, if these classes are too far away for you, there are other options. Check continuing education programs to see if classes are offered. Community arts centers usually have crafts people who give classes. Local artists will usually be your best source of information for how to get started.

Augusta Heritage Workshop (Elkins) is offered annually in July and August. Courses are given in an adult camp setting, making the stay there a working vacation. Past offerings have included beginning and

43

intermediate classes, stained glass painting, glass etching and sandblasting.

Cedar Lake Craft Center in Ripley offers intensive, week-long classes in summer, and weekend workshops are in fall, spring, and winter. Past classes have included beginning and advanced stained glass, mirrors and overlays, and sandblasting and classes in related areas such as beginning and intermediate design and creativity classes.

Headwinds in Parkersburg offers classes taught by Morningstar White and makes supplies available.

Huntington Galleries in Huntington not only offers occasional classes, it also promotes and exhibits contemporary glass, making it a great place to get ideas about the kind of work you might want to do.

Shobes Glass in Huntington is a source of classes and supplies. Call toll-free 800-642-3586.

Nancy Williams Snodgrass in Charleston. Call 768-0549.

Materials: Getting the Right Stuff

West Virginia is close to many of the best glass factories, a proximity which affords a special opportunity to go directly to the glassmakers. Visiting supply houses lets you see glass and determine exact needs. Most supply houses will try to match glass if you send a sample. Ordering by mail or telephone, you can shop for best prices, particularly for solder, lead came, copper foil, molds, etc.

Blenko Glass Company, Milton. Blenko is famous for its antique glass and lovely dalle de verre. They also sell scrap glass for 90¢ per pound, a real deal for this quality glass!

D&L Stained Glass, Boulder, CO. 1-800-525-0940.

Franklin Art Glass, German Village, Columbus, OH. 1-800-227-8920.

Nervo International, 650 University Ave., Berkeley, CA 94710.

Prism Art Glass, West Liberty, OH.

Shobes Stained Glass Supply, 1529 4th Ave., Huntington, WV 25701. 1-800-642-3586.

Wismach Glass Company, Paden City, WV.

Keeping It Going

Stained glass artists find that although books may help one work out specific problems, "design ideas come from everywhere," as Hight says. "Books, magazines, walking outside, just looking at anything and everything." They suggested several favorite sources: *How to Work in Stained Glass,* by Anita and Seymour Isenberg (Chilton Books); *New Glass,* by Otto Rigan (Ballantine Books); *Tiffany Windows,* by Alastair Duncan (Simon and Schuster); *Stained Glass,* by Lawrence Lee and others (Crown Publishing); *Ludwig Schaffrath: Stained Glass and Mosaic,* by Konrad Stephany; and *Drawing on the Right Side of the Brain,* by Betty Edwards (Tarcher).

Magazines and Newsletters

The American Art Glass Quarterly, 2698 Marine Way, Mountain View, CA 94043.

American Craft Council, P.O. Box 1308 CL, Fort Lee, NJ 07024.

Art Craft Magazine, 324 Datura Street, West Palm Beach, FL 33401.

Glass Studio, P.O. Box 23383, Portland, OR 97223.

Stained Glass Magazine (published by the Stained Glass Association of America), 1125 Wilmington Ave., St. Louis, MO 63111.

Sculpture:
So Pure and Physical

Martha Miles

"I am reclusive. My inspiration comes from my family, my close friends, and the world around me, most particularly my world at Bear Wallow Ridge. I prefer to work with natural materials—wood and stone. I use a chisel and mallet. The work is slow and tedious, but so pure and physical—exhilarating—like the gratifying feeling you get after a strenuous run," writes Susan Wood.

Sculpture has long been considered a man's art form. Now, however, women have not only broken into the field, but have created a particularly female place for themselves in sculpture. The sculptors represented here reflect the sense of themselves as female sculptors. Diana Wohl, formerly from West Virginia and now living in Ohio, won the Governor's Merit Award for sculpture. She puts her experience like this:

"I have a feeling that there is something intrinsically female about my approach to woodcarving. Defining and then dissolving the boundaries between subject and object and reassembling the elements into a new whole may indicate an attempt to recreate that primordial infant-like and pre-infant-like state where there is no boundary between the experiencer and the experienced. Neither the process nor the resulting sculpture expresses an analysis of experience, which seems traditionally to be the nature of masculine art. Female art attempts to address not what life means but what life is."

Susan Wood, an extensive exhibitor, says that she "matured as an artist and a woman in the West Virginia Appalachians." She also talks about the problem of being a woman in a male-dominated field.

"I am not ignorant of my position as a female sculptor in a male sculptor's world, and I shall fight for my recognition as an artist. I have often felt the isolation of being the only woman sculptor invited to symposia, gallery workshops and showings. I reject stereotyped judgments based upon sexual inferiority. I want to be challenged and judged as an individual. My work is different—not readily acceptable. Perhaps this is why I have matured and work best in West Virginia. Despite the sexual bias inherent in this rural, semi-Southern region, the indigenous culture demands that you prove yourself first as an individual. It is ultimately supportive."

Diane McCartney of Morgantown discusses why sculpting is part of her life: "The physical handling of the clay and the building of the armature along with the knowledge of anatomy and the talent for capturing the likeness of the subject bring on a 'high' for the sculptor as the work progresses. The senses of touch and sight become more acute. An overwhelming attitude of awareness, spiritual in nature, blends with the mental and physical to make sculpting an exhausting, exciting, rewarding adventure."

Art and Family

Each of the four sculptors discusses the problem faced by women trying to combine marriage, children and career. Most decisive is Alison Helm, a faculty member at WVU's College of Creative Arts and a winner of the Governor's Award, who advises, "Don't try and have a full-fledged family life and have a professional career in art. Sometimes the two don't mix unless you are already established. It's difficult to have children when you are young and still have time enough to devote to your art work."

McCartney, a classical sculptor, sees the problem in retrospect. With four children and a house to care for, "ninety percent of the time, the art came second." Now that her last child is in college, a time she foresaw as her chance to focus on her art, her mother, elderly and not well, is living with them. None of these sculptors, however, regrets their decisions or find that children and marriage are less worthy endeavors than art.

Wohl, who calls herself "always an artist, always a mother," has given this problem a great deal of thought. "The most reassuring realization I've come upon is that for five years I've been both a mother and a sculptor, and I will always be both. When I am most involved in nurturing my children, even though I'm not wielding a mallet, I am learning about love and life and change and innocence. What I experience in mothering gives my thoughts maturity and my creativity substance. And when my children no longer need my full attention, I'm sure that those qualities I've developed to meet the needs of motherhood will always exist to enrich my art. Perhaps I'm beginning to treat my wood like I treat my children—and my children so far have turned out fine."

Wood says much the same thing:

"I am an artist. I am a wife. I am a mother. All these roles are a necessary part of all that I am. I have always sought to achieve a balance between my life and work, but conflict is inevitable. I have had to learn to establish priorities, to develop disciplines, to overcome pain and obstacles, to be patient. I am not always successful. My children and husband came first as they needed me, but my work was always there." Speaking of her husband, also an artist, she says, "I could not be all that I am without my husband."

Making a Living

How do sculptors make a living? Wohl has one answer:

"To support woodcarving, an artist has to broaden her skills. I've found that learning carpentry skills gives me a much wider range of financially-viable activities. Women with carpentry skills can make furniture, toys, utensils, and combine these activities with sculptural designs. Also, I've used my carpentry skills frequently in building theatre sets."

How to Learn

McCartney meticulously kept a notebook when she was working on her first sculpture, then went back later and starred the notations that would help in the future, reducing trial and error. Her notebook includes comments about where the children were and what happened when she didn't make the blue plaster layer thick enough.

Alison Helm

Wohl advises beginners to buy a good technical woodcarving book, one that discusses the maintenance and proper use of tools as well as specific carpentry skills. On learning, she says, "There is something quaintly medieval about learning woodworking. The most significant learning experiences for me have come from master/apprentice relationships. The times I've found someone, usually a retired carpenter, to take the time to teach me a few of his techniques and tricks of the trade have been the experiences which have essentially shaped my woodworking skills from these encounters, but I have been privileged to get to know some practical-minded, salt-of-the-earth characters. Sometimes a good story is worth a dozen explanations."

Practical Matters

Workspace

For those working with plaster, McCartney advises working outside with buckets and tubs, as most plumbing will not handle plaster. Wohl says, "For larger projects where my basement proved inadequate both in terms of space and facilities, I found the industrial arts department of a local college very willing to let me use its facilities with some special arrangements for access and insurance." Susan Wood uses two rooms and a loft, 300 yards from home. She has four 12 x 16' desk and work tables, a 4 x 12' storage sink and stove. She uses natural fluorescent lighting, and she has a separate area for plaster, away from wax and clay. She and her husband are building an addition to the studio that will include a foundry with burnout kiln, furnace and additional storage.

Supplies and Tools

Wohl lists her necessary supplies: "In addition to a large table with an appropriate vise, a slow acquisition of tools, both hand and power tools, is a must. Over the years I've found a saber saw, industrial grinder, electrical drill, drill press, router, bandsaw and chainsaw to be particularly useful. A variety of high-quality chisels and gouges are also essential. Also in the space set up for woodcarving, there must be a corner for letting wood sit and dry out for a long period of time—years."

Promotion

"Eighty percent of my work has been given away, five percent has been sold, fifteen percent is under my bed and very little has been shown," comments Diane McCartney. "I had better learn more about this (promotion)." Wohl says, "I'm basically selfish when it comes to woodcarving. I do it primarily for myself, not for the public. Realistically, this is not a particularly marketable approach to art. I'm not too interested in selling my pieces right now, but I think it is important for them to be seen. I enter a lot of shows and try to show my work in various galleries. My goal is to keep something in public at all times."

Wood also promotes herself seriously. She had business cards designed by a professional graphic artist and feels that the cards are essential. She also points out that a sculptor gets good name recognition from shows. She has a tax advisor in conjunction with a family business.

What I experience in mothering gives my thoughts maturity and my creativity substance.

—Diana Wohl

Resources for Sculptors

Tools
Sculptor House (also a good source for plasticene), 38 East 30th Street, New York, NY 10016.

Sculpture Associates, 40 East 19th Street, New York, NY 10003 (212) 777-2400.

Wood
Lumber yards, locally.

Clay
Standard Ceramic Supply Co., P.O. Box 4435, Pittsburgh, PA 15205-4435.

Columbus Clay Co., 1205 East 17th Avenue, Columbus, OH 43211.

Wax
A-Kindt Collins, 12651 Elmwood Avenue, Cleveland, OH 44111.

Bronze
R. Lavins & Sons, Inc., 3426 S. Kedzie Avenue, Chicago, IL.

Mold
Perma-Flex Mold Co., 1919 E. Livingston Avenue, Columbus, OH 43209.

Sand
Millwood Sand, Zanesville, OH.

Bibliography

Books:
Brenda Putnam, *The Sculptor's Way*
James Dunlop, *Anatomical Diagrams*
Bernard Leach, *A Potter's Book*
Cindy Nemser, *Art Talk*

Journals
Art in America, 488 Madison Avenue, New York, NY 10022
New Art Examiner, 230 East Ohio, Chicago, IL 60611
Sculpture Review, 15 East 26th Street, New York, NY 10010
Sculptors International, International Sculpture Center, P.O. Box 19709, Washington, D.C. 20036
The Quality Crafts Market, 521 Fifth Avenue, Suite 1700, New York, NY 10017

Dance:

Even on the Ground the Dancer Takes the Air

Gail Adams

Gail Adams

I am a dancer who no longer does. I am the toes tapping on the bottom of the concert seat, the torso slowly rolling as the dancer on the stage makes mad swings; the exaggerated yawn ending in a stretch-contract. Starting out a dancer, along the way I changed, but I hope to keep the rhythm of the ways.

When one who has been trained in the classical way thinks of dance, the five positions are central. These basic cornerstones of ballet and modern dance are outwardly simple, deceptively difficult, impossible to explain. In first position, the heels are touched together—that seems enough. Is there a way to convey the turned-out leg, the pulled-up arch that marks the novice from one who knows to line the knee above the toe when one pliés?

"I've been dancing all my life. The most interesting and I think surprising discovery," writes Joy Lurie Friedlander, a dancer-choreographer affiliated with Point Park College in Pittsburgh and Director of the 1984 Northeast Regional College Dance Festival, "was and still is, how much more there is to learn. The qualities of movement are infinite."

Friedlander continues, "To really become a dancer, a person must understand what they are dancing, and not just how they look and what to do next. This takes each person a different time to discover. I found my true dancing self after I began choreographing my own work."

"I mainly dance for myself now," writes Adrienne Biesemeyer of Alderson. A well-known fiber artist, she notes, "when I was active most of my time was spent in choreography. I do a half-hour of general exercise each morning now, then on odd days it runs into an hour and a half."

Second position is a generous one; the straddle stance, the arms outstretched, the sideways lap, the possibility of leap are all promised. Second is the one to start out in.

"Dance movement therapy is psychotherapy which uses movement to help patients heal themselves," informs Florette Orleans, a dance therapist from Clarksburg. "Using the structure of the circle, touch rhythm, and verbal imagery, dance can help the severely disturbed experience, if only momentarily, a coming together of self. Using the motions of everyday life—walking, bending, jumping, reaching, turning, this dance movement lets each patient realize immediate success."

Third position is always difficult. Lining the heel up with the opposite instep can be done, but keeping the proper turn out and keeping the tuck as one plies is hard. My feet seemed to yearn for each other; they were anticipating fifth and were not satisfied with halfway there.

Artistic director Michael Pedretti of The International Movement Theatre at Davis and Elkins College in Elkins is emphatic about the necessity of movement and its importance in life. "All people must dance or die. To discourage an individual not to dance because he/she may never make a living at the box office is to fall victim to our commercial world."

Fourth is a stance beloved by jazz and modern dancers and exuberant walkers. It is a striding step and here is how to do it. From a second position put your right foot out in front. Now you are standing in a freize design but forget flat and turn both feet so they look out—away from the center of your spine. A trick to tell if you are lined up is this: Step back quickly with your right foot and the heel should dovetail nicely against the toe of the left. A lunge, a fencer's love, a grand touche; fourth is a pose perfect to lean from, extend into an arabesque, kick back and forth in a crazed can-can.

"The question for me," asks Sharon Goodman, an artist who considers movement central to her drawing, "is why doesn't everyone dance? I really don't understand why everyone doesn't share my passion for dancing. In middle age I found ballet too technical and rigorous to enjoy so I switched allegiance to folk dancing because you don't have to be a trained dancer to enjoy folk. You only need to be persistent. I love the music, the variety of movement, the people attracted to the form. But most of all I love learning the dances and dancing them well."

The last postion is fifth. The tightest, the most difficult, the one that when you have the turnout is a triumph. Heel to toe, toe to heel, your feet are two sardines wedged into one can. From here you explode like a magic trick—huge streamers flying up from an uncorked jar. As you rise into the air your feet beat wildly for their freedom. "See," fifth says, "I've fooled you. This is not one large foot and one fat leg but two, and they can take the air." Then once again demure, they land. The dance in form resembles all the tools of dance. Toeshoes, improbably fragile looking, palest pink satin are really built up layers of wood, leather, glue, hard boxes into which a dancer slides a foot to stand *en pointe*.

This compression, this hidden identity of dance is what intrigues. Carving out hours of practice and the art of carving are fused in the art of Jude Binder of The Heartwood Dance Center in Big Bend. "My focus in dance is on its use as a tool for personal growth, health and happiness. I see it as a healing as well as a performing art. I'm the same person when I carve or dance. I see the same things and have the same responses. I see tremendous connections between wood, flesh and spirit. I feel that in carving, dancing or teaching I'm learning the same lessons, following the same principles and pursuing my potential."

Fiona Morris, Director of the Morgantown School of Ballet, discussed what qualities a young person needs in order to dance: "I think a well-proportioned body and coordination, as well as the ability to concentrate and retain certain dance steps. But it's no good just being able to copy. First, they have to enjoy dance, simply because of the movement and the music. A gifted student is musical and has a natural sense of time, space, and awareness of his or her own body."

Now I am the bare sole sensibly shod, yet still my toes fan and curl before sleep. The only thing that dancers rarely care for is their feet; it is assumed that when all else creaks and strains, those two will shuffle on. When I wriggle my toes, cross the second over the big, they still make a double shelf that helps a dancer hobble without bunny pads. Unused their broken ends seem sad. When I was a dancer the bottoms of my feet were as hard and yellow as the varnished wood floors they moved on, and callouses grew so thick they interfered with balance; trimming was a ritual. There is an art to paring down corns with razor blades, slicing horny flesh as a cheese plane pulls off rind.

I know too, that if there is a blister it is best to leave it alone until the flesh goes from bleeding pink to the color of biscuits. Then the skin can be pinched up and torn to the side leaving a perfect round. There is no weeping from the flesh because the underneath has grown, is able to support weight again.

So a dancer's body changes, only flesh and fragile as all humans are; and yet the bones, the muscle and the desire to dance, to see, talk and write about dance is strong. Even on the ground the dancer takes the air.

Beginning A Life In Dance

"Primarily I'm a teacher. Teaching grounds me and gives me the opportunity to share my experience in the art. Without it I'd be lonely and floating." Binder sees visual arts and dance as activities that enhance each other. "My favorite work in the visual arts is woodcarving because the beauty and malleability of the wood is so compelling." Teaching taught Binder "creativity is a universally natural thing that becomes obstructed and distorted...even young children display painful self-consciousness in the creative arts." She echoes Pedretti, saying "injection of competition in creative activity is detrimental, interrupting full communication with the self, and it's there with the self, that the artist in one resides." It's the teacher's job she believes "to set the stage for this contact with the self, to provide the environment and materials, make her own skills available for reference and offer optimistic encouragement."

"I think," answers Biesemeyer, "it is important to let kids hear all kinds of music, be free and unstructured for the first five years—then structure will come. Often dance is taught as form and movement that are just athletic, not classical or mystical—too often it is taught in a gym."

Pedretti agrees. "To dance (move creatively) is natural. To express oneself through movement is as much a part of life as to breathe. Only in a competitive American society must youth think that this dance has to be expressed only in competitive sports like soccer, football, baseball, etc."

"Creative movement is a natural form of self-expression for the child," says Joy Faini Saab of WVU, "since we know that much of a child's self esteem is based on what he or she can do. I don't believe in rehearsing small children for a fully-costumed stage revue." Saab feels each child needs time to become aware of his or her own body and what it is able to do. "There will always be time for children to share what they are learning with parents and friends," but she stresses, "the emphasis must not be on the perfected sequence but on how children begin to know all the ways they can move."

Friedlander notes "although many private dance school teachers are not thoroughly trained to teach, a good many of them give future dancers their initial motivation. One's first dance teacher is so important as he/she either instills or discourages the passion for dance."

Primarily I'm a teacher. Teaching grounds me and gives me the opportunity to share my experience in the art. Without it I'd be lonely and floating.

—Jude Binder

Morris remembers vividly a performance in London". . . we demonstrated Royal Academy exam work. The whole thing was very exciting, everyone warming up backstage, putting on make-up, peeling off leg warmers. There's a certain smell, of the stage, of resin . . . we got shouted at to keep quiet, we were so exhilarated. And I made up my mind then to go on stage."

She says, "Of course as a teacher I look for potential professional ballet dancers, but most youngsters come to take class because they love ballet. It's closely related to music and drama, and with its historical and national heritages it gives a well-balanced education as well as helping to develop mind and body."

Earlier Friedlander noted that teachers who are not carefully trained in dance are becoming more aware of what constitutes good dance, although she cautions "many bad habits are picked up by students from these instructors, and all have to be unlearned later." Morris concurs, noting most excesses begin with *pointe* work begun too early. "If a young girl has been studying seriously for two to three years, that is, at least two classes per week, I would consider starting her *en pointe*. Only then if she had acquired strength throughout her body and muscular control, as well as a good understanding of the *relevé* and *demi-pointe* work. Also, she should be around 11 or 12 years of age, as only then are the bones of the foot and ankle well formed."

Kristen Brandt-McDaniel, Artistic Director of West Virginia University's Ballet Ensemble credits Susan Abbey Sherman, original founder of the WVU Ballet Program, as an important influence in her teaching style. Also an inspiration for Brandt-McDaniel was Wang Shao-Pen, Ballet Master at The School of the Hartford Ballet where she received her teacher's certificate in dance. This respected school follows a program strictly modeled on Kirov Ballet pedagogy and "this rigidity could have been stifling." But Shao-Pen's fresh imagery and gentle movements made him an exemplary teacher. "He'd softly touch a tense student and say 'Don't worry, it's easy,' and it would be then."

A unique opportunity is offered to older dancers at WVU through Orchesis sponsor Mary Katherine Wiedebusch who has arranged, for the past several years, a series of nationally-known guest artists in dance.

Rick Lee/WV Department of Culture and History

Orchesis

Wiedebusch speaks for all dance teachers when she affirms: "A student must want to dance well because that is half the accomplishment. I urge them to be dedicated and unselfish and to be ready for plenty of hard work. It pays off in the end."

Classes like Wiedebusch's, Brandt-McDaniel's, and Linda Plavin's Mountain Jazz Dance Theatre instruct those of college age, but what of those who want to begin dance in their more mature years?

Pedretti sees an expansion of the idea of dance as a way to allow one to practice the art for a lifetime. "The School for Movement Theatre program considers the idea of dance with movement to be enlarged to include puppetry, mime, and clowning."

Friedlander asserts, "I don't believe it's too late to begin—EVER! It's unlikely a 40-year-old beginner will become a professional performer, but the benefits of dance—learning rhythm, coordination, musicality—and its joy—make it always a worthwhile beginning."

Reverence

Webster's dictionary defines reverence as a respect felt or shown, a profound adoring, a deep emotion or regard, but to dancers it means the end of class. At the end of every classical ballet class, and many modern ones, there is the ritual of reverence. It is a formal exercise that consists of *port de bras*, gracious acknowledgment of a nonexistent audience and always deep and sweeping bows, delicious to perform. Here is where one honors dance, its discipline, its history, its grace.

"I began my formal training in dance as a ballet student in Washington, DC, studying the Cechetti method with Lisa Gardiner and Mary Day," recalls Binder. "I was nine years old and remember the first time I stood at the *barre* and turned out my legs. I feel connected to that little girl everytime I place my hand on the *barre* and stand to."

"By age five, dance was a part of my life and at age seven I began to study modern dance with Savilla Fort and ballet at the American School of Ballet," writes Biesemeyer. "My favorite dancers are Savill— that first modern teacher, Katherine Dunham, my six-year-old daughter and my sisters Gina and Shari." She remembers too a performance by Pilobolus as well as memorable performances by the Winnipeg Ballet Company and Alvin Ailey.

Goodman thanks dance for "two wonderful things it gives to me. The most important is the release of tension from physical activity. I always feel revived after dancing no matter how tired I was before; it's hard to be concerned about things when one is dancing with all one's heart. The second thing is that when I dance I don't have to think about being creative. I only have to learn my steps and learn them well. As a visual artist I am always striving for new and more profound images. Dance affords me the luxury of not having to think creatively, of total relaxation and enjoyment. Yet, it is a major influence in my art. My passion for dance feeds and finds its way into my drawings and paintings which are concerned with movement."

Dance offers me the luxury of not having to think creatively, of total relaxation and enjoyment.

—Sharon Goodman

I recall that after each last bow, a pause, the applause for a class well taught, well learned, my image met my eye. I was always surprised to see a face I recognized.

—Gail Adams

West Virginia and Region: Dance Opportunities/Companies

A complete list of dance companies can be obtained from the Cultural Center in Charleston.

"West Virginia's air of creativity is certainly a powerful stimulus for creative work. People studying at MTI refer to West Virginia as "that magical, almost therapeutic air that stimulates us to do our best work," says Pedretti.

Annual Dance Festival of West Virginia. Held in Charleston. Sponsored by the Cultural Center. Contact Barbara Phillips.

Debbie Beckward and Company, 480 View Ave, Fairmont. Debbie and company performed a Career Dance Workshop at Fairmont State during Black History Week.

Camp Washington Carver Choreographic Workshop. A summer workshop for WV choreographers, offered sporadically.

Dance in the Valley, Coolfont Recreation Center, Berkeley Springs. This weeklong workshop usually held in June is a project of the Washington, DC Joy of Motion Dance Center. A nonprofit and tax-exempt arts organization, JOM has done a residency at Coolfont for the past seven years. Classes are held in the Coolfont entertainment barn. Single classes are open at a rate of $5.00 per day. Various dance approaches including Cechetti and Graham are offered.

Heartwood Dance Center: Dance in the Hills Route 1 Box 61, Big Bend, 26136. Jude Binder, Director. This nonprofit dance center offers classes in ballet, modern and jazz. Located in Calhoun County the center offers traditional dance approaches and opportunity for students to explore creative movement. Binder also makes "beautiful little dance shapes, bodies in metals."

Jerry Rose Dance Company, 107 McTaggart Drive, Beckley, 25801. Jerry and Sherry Rose, Directors. Both Adrienne Biesemeyer and Michael Pedretti noted the excellence of teaching offered by the Roses.

Morgantown Ballet, 429 Beechurst Avenue, Morgantown, 26505. Fiona Morris, Director. With a long reputation for excellence, the Morgantown School of Ballet continues to uphold its reputation.

Mountain Jazz Dance Theatre, 115 E. Moore Hall, WVU, Morgantown, 26505. Linda Plavin, Artistic Director. Mountain Jazz Dance Theatre consists of 19 performers selected by open audition. Course credit at WVU is optional. Plavin teaches all levels of jazz technique in addition to choreography and dance composition. She also devises balance beam and floor exercises for the WVU Varsity Women's Gymnastics Team and gives lecture-demonstrations in dance history with special emphasis on the 1920's.

Orchesis, E. Moore Hall, WVU, Morgantown, 26506. Mary Katherine Wiedebusch, Artistic Director. Wiedebusch notes of the residencies of professional artists/dancers that make prize-winning choreography possible: "It is an unique opportunity for our dancers."

This compression,
this hidden identity of dance
is what intrigues.

The School for Movement Theatre-International, c/o Davis and Elkins College, Elkins, 26241. Michael Pedretti, Artistic Director. "The best teachers in their areas of specialty come from all over the world—an entire Kathakali company in 1982 and 1983 to share their perceptions, skills and personal approach." Pedretti also notes that classes are limited to 20 with many having fewer than 15.

West Virginia University Ballet Ensemble. 207 Coliseum, WVU, Morgantown, 26505. Kristen Brandt-McDaniel, Artistic Director.
Brandt-McDaniel's Ballet Ensemble is composed of dedicated student dancers of whom she says, "They're doing it because they love dance. And it takes a lot of time to do it." She is interested in further developing the preparatory ballet class program and sees lecture-demonstrations in the public schools as an excellent way to introduce dance to West Virginians.

Point Park College, Dance Division of the Department of Fine, Applied and Performing Arts. 412-765-2336. Point Park College was the site and hosted the NERDF Por 1984. This is a festival sponsored by the American College Dance Festival Association and offers college student choreographers an opportunity to both present, perform and learn from choreographers and national dance figures. Both workshops and concert were open to the public with a limited number of observation tickets available.

Dance Resources/Bibliography/Organizations
National Dance Opportunities
American Dance Festival, Box 6097, College Station, Durham, NC 27708. The ADF holds a six week summer session annually. 1984 marked its 50th anniversary.

Dance Critics' Conference, c/o American Dance Festival, Box 6097. Write Special Projects Coordinator. Tuition is $500 and sponsorship from a newspaper is needed. Write for further details.

Jacob's Pillow Dance Festival, Box 287, Lee, MA, 01238.
An annual eight-week summer program. Michael Pedretti suggests both this and ADF noting they "have excellent classes but somewhat narrower vision" than programs emphasizing extended curriculum.

National Association of Regional Ballet, 1860 Broadway, NY, NY 10023. Provides *Dance/America*, a *Newsletter*, information on festivals, conferences, choreographers, dance tours, set, and costume.

Bibliography

This listing is both representative and subjective, reflecting the personal choices of those who replied to the questionnaire.

Books

Joan Brady. *The Unmaking of a Dancer*. Harper Row, 1982. Excellent autobiography about a dancer who left dancing and then retrained in her mid-thirties just to see if she would be able to be a dancer again. Interesting and touching.

Arlene Croce. *After-Images*. Random House, 1979, and *Going to the Dance*, New York: Knopf 1982.

Agnes DeMille: *Dance to the Piper; And Promenade Home; Dance to Me, Speak to Me;* and *Reprieve; A Memoir*.
All of DeMille's books are worth reading because hers is a life lived for dance, and uniquely American dance.

Edwin Denby. *Looking at the Dance*, and *Dancers, Buildings and People in the Street*.
Both wonderful books on dance—well written essays.

Isadora Duncan. *My Life*. NY: Liveright, 1955.

Katherine Dunham. *A Touch of Innocence*. 1959.
This focuses on Dunham's early years rather than her dancing life but is wonderful reading.

Margot Fonteyn. *Autobiography*. New York: Knopf, 1976.
Friedlander notes this "is a wonderful for anyone."

The Notebooks of Martha Graham. Introduction by Nancy Wilson Ross. (NY: Harcourt Brace, 1973). Not as instructive on the dancer as many other biographies, but some insight into creative process. To see "x bali x bali x kneel circle holding snake" helps one to visualize the process of making dances.

Doris Humphrey. *The Art of Making Dances*. New York: Rinehart, 1959. Wonderful work on choreography.

Myron Nadel and Constance Miller, eds. *The Dance Experience: Readings in Dance Appreciation*. Universe Press, 1978. Nadel is an associate professor of dance at Carnegie Mellon.

Dance Directory: Programs of Professional Preparation in American Colleges and Universities. 11th edition, 1980. American Association of Dance Educators. Check and see if updated edition is now out. An invaluable source.

Dance Magazine. 1180 Avenue of Americas, NY, NY 10036. The single best source of information on dance. Begin here with a subscription.

The only thing that dancers rarely care for is their feet.
It is assumed that when all else creaks and strains, those two will shuffle on.

—Gail Adams

Theatre:

I Learn Lines in the Car

Ann Miller

Shakespeare Theatre

"Theatre," says Denise Huot, "gives one a safe chance to do a lot of outrageous things one wouldn't dare to do in everyday life."

Through interviewing people like Huot, I have met many creative women. These organizers, performers, puppeteers, singers, actors, writers and directors—all of them are doers.

I had lived in West Virginia only a short time when I was asked to gather together this theatre section. How to do it, when although I love theatre in all of its guises, I knew little of theatre here.

I decided to simply let these women speak for themselves, as in various ways they attempted to answer my questions—How did you get started? How do you keep going? How do you get it out?

Bonnie Brown, actor and state legislator, found that the women's movement changed her thinking about theatre. For International Women's Year in 1977, she created, along with other women, a group which later became the Women's Repertory Theatre of West Virginia.

Brown writes, "After I had became involved in the women's movement, my thoughts about theatre changed, as I too was undergoing a transition. The roles for women were sparse and many times stereotypes. For close to a year, several men and women met on a weekly basis to talk about alternative theatre in Charleston. Many ideas evolved, but nothing got off the ground.

"I knew by this time that I really wanted a women's theatre. I wanted to fuse the two major interests of mine, theatre and women's rights. I wanted a message to be brought forth, but wasn't sure how to go about doing it."

The group is still viable, Brown says, and "will rise to the occasion should it arise. One of the beauties of our theatre is simplicity, which allows for setting up in small places end eases our travel. The props fit into a couple of boxes and the set usually consists of tables and stools or chairs."

The *grande dame* of innovative theatre may well be Maryat Lee, who lives, works, and writes in Hinton. There in the hills her EcoTheatre, of which she is founder and playwright, producer and director.

What is EcoTheatre? In Lee's words, "a place for *seeing*, ourselves and our home. It is both a mirror and a window, and sometimes a door."

Lee frequently works with what would seem to be the most unpromising material and the most unlikely staff. She began her project using disadvantaged teenagers as actors. Yet this practice is totally in keeping with her philosophy of theatre as "the experience of *being* in a disciplined framework—a mighty experience for both subject and spectator.

"For us theatre is an occasion, if you will, for the actor to be truly seen, as we are rarely seen in this life. And when it happens, it is impossible not to celebrate.

"What I want in the theatre (which originally, of course, was the church) is just this—'Here I am!' in all the facets and analogues and meanings that we are capable of seeing. When it is present, the past is present, the future is present, the word becomes flesh, the invisible is made visible, a door opens to another world, and the actor and audience find a communion based on truth, not a trick or a lie.

"The theatre takes on the meaning of a sacrament when, from time to time, almost by accident or grace, the actor is there, vulnerable, exposed and we say, 'He did it' or 'She did it,' and we experience this with gratitude and love. I know that this experience seems to happen to a few of the very great actors who seem to transcend all kinds of barriers, but it can also happen to plain people, when they take the risk. And it takes away one's breath."

What Lee advocates is nothing short of redefinition. "Go slow but steady," she advises. "The theatre field does not need one more group following the professional models. What is needed are people who start from scratch and redefine theatre from top to bottom."

And this she says to anyone trying to write for the theatre: "Whatever you do, make sure that your writing is as regular as brushing your teeth. It has to be a habit that comes before anything else. Plan also for your recreation. There has to be a time to regroup, relax, and enjoy others."

She does recommend working at home. "Many times you will find that in the middle of the night you will have the need to write or work on a problem, or the solution to a problem will make itself known to you. It is also important to have someone around to help you with the phone and to direct problems or interruptions away from you during your creative work time. Let it be known that you do not wish to be bothered during those times unless it is a real emergency."

Joann Spencer Siegrist, for twelve years director of the WVU Puppet Mobile, is another innovator. Siegrist also does solo performing and runs her own private company, The Puppet Planter. She is in charge of the puppetry, children's theatre, and creative drama programs at WVU.

"Creative abilities are in everyone," she says, but "the largest difference for productivity and satisfaction comes from confidence. Anything that stems from our creative core must be nurtured with confidence so the result of the creative energies is not allowed to weaken or ebb into a weak dream or compromise.

"You must be organized but relaxingly flexible." She exhibits that combination of traits herself in the way she finds and creates her equipment, as she says, "everywhere, constantly! Fabrics and craft stores, yard and garage sales, hardware and lumber stores—you name it. I just built a portable puppet stage from a lawnmower grass collector."

Another innovator, Denise Huot of Pittsburgh has appeared on Broadway and Off-Broadway. Trained at Carnegie-Mellon University and the London Academy of Music and Dramatic Art, she has also performed for television, radio, and film. She tells first why theatre appeals so much to her.

"It is energy-lifting, exciting, hard work and the demands are great. Excellent for keeping mentally alert and physically in good shape."

But it is in the personality that she finds rewards. "Even though an actor is a *re*-creator (the playwright is the creator), there is still much scope for study of another personality. I find the study fascinating and enjoy finding strengths, quirks, nuances, etc., and then 'trying them on.'

"The big bonus boost for me is when people from the audience say the characters were like real people, and that their thoughts and feelings were clear. Acting is a bit like being Sherlock Holmes—unearthing all the playwright's clues and solving the mystery."

Kate Young is an actor and singer who has appeared both with symphony orchestras and in regional theatre. A specialist in early music, the Elizabethan period, and concert narration, Young is a graduate of Brown University and the University of Pittsburgh. Young lives in Wheeling but commutes to Pittsburgh to teach and perform. As she told a reporter for the Pittsburgh *Post-Gazette*, "A lot of people told me I wouldn't be able to have a career and live in Wheeling, which I am discovering is not true. A lot of career opportunities are opening up for me now, and if I can work out the scheduling and my husband understands, I can do it."

Young now says, "I found that it is possible to make your life and career anywhere you choose if you have flexibility, stamina, drive and determination. I only regret the lack of professional union theatre in the state, and that I must work out of state in my field.

"I am sure my career would be quite different in a major cultural center in the states or in Europe, but I doubt whether I would have developed the flexibility, drive, and versatility, nor found such diversity or such beauty elsewhere."

It is both a mirror and a window,
and sometimes a door.

—Maryat Lee

Jeanne Schramm as Clara Barton

Jeanne Schramm, a reference librarian at West Liberty State College, got into acting through research. In 1979, when the Susan B. Anthony dollar was issued, she thought she'd better be prepared for all those students who would be doing their term papers on Anthony. "But no one ever came; no one was interested." So Schramm simply sat down and read the information she had gathered. There she met a fascinating woman through her own words. Far from the hard, humorless image Anthony has been burdened with, Schramm found a likable, witty, caring but determined woman.

Schramm plunged right into one-woman shows with her compilation of Anthony's letters, speeches and articles. Since that time she has received more than 200 invitations to perform in 14 states. Her other portrayals are Clara Barton, Julia Ward Howe, Harriet Beecher Stowe and Dorothea Dix. "When I'm choosing a character to portray," Schramm once said, "I try to pick shakers and movers, women who have really accomplished something. And I like to choose characters from the 19th century, women who were involved in social issues of the time—slavery, suffrage, mental health."

Schramm, who gave her first performance when she was 38, had no previous experience in theatre nor any training in it. She learned, she says, by observing others' techniques and following Marlon Brando's advice: "Make it appear as though you have no idea what you're going to say next." She has no agent, writer, or publicist. She researches and writes her scripts, puts together her costumes, designs posters, writes publicity material, and contracts for her own bookings.

"I select only those women whose lives have changed the world. I select passages which I find particularly moving and meaningful."

Schramm says of all the women she portrays, she feels closest to Susan B. Anthony. Her presentation describes the pain, humiliation and

I learn lines in the car,
and the truck drivers sometimes
look at me kind of funny.
—Kate Young

injustice endured by women of Anthony's time. "Those benefitting from the new rights have absoutely no idea where any of it came from," she says. "They don't know the suffering. They don't know the sacrifice. They don't know what it has cost other women. Perhaps one day they will."

Publicity

Denise Huot suggests: Include an 8" x 10" glossy, black and white headshot with resume (same size, firmly attached to one side.) Use a photographer who does commercial and publicity shots. Use postcards, with photo, to remind people who you are. Have an answering machine or answering service. A missed phone call can mean a missed audition or job. Be prepared to spend a lot on postage, copying, photography and long distance phone calls. It's still nearly impossible though, to market yourself by yourself. Simply isn't time. Actors get tax-audited a lot—especially when they do well financially in any one year. Keep EVERYTHING! Every slip, receipt, chitty, that you even suspect might be deductible as a working expense.

Resources

The "Resources" section of this book lists many theatre groups and organizations.

Pittsburgh Post/Gazette

Kate Young

Classical Music:

Nothing Could Have Taken Its Place in My Life

Susan Williams

Consuelo Sherba, whose parents both loved music, remembers "longing to listen to classical music from a very early age." She also read biographies of musicians when she was a child. "They were charming books and I got excited about the travel they spoke of."

Sherba began playing piano at age five in her home in New York. At age 12, "late to be starting," she began playing violin. In New York, she attended the High School of Music and Art, City College, where she studied with Felix Galimar, and she later studied viola at the University of Wisconsin with Bernard Zaslav and at the University of Massachusetts with Philip Maegele. Among her first and most important teachers were Thruston Johnson and Blanche Swartz Levy. She has played with the Budapest Quartet and the Fine Arts Quartet of Cleveland.

She tells young people wanting to go into music that they must be "enormously dedicated. Don't just think, 'This is fun and I'm kind of good at it.' This is a highly competitive field. There are more and more good people going into it. Be honest with yourself. Assess how much you enjoy your music and how much talent you have. Trust the person you study with. Build a solid foundation. And be sure you enjoy music; if you don't enjoy you won't enjoy it later when there's more pressure."

Her husband is also a musician. "That's a plus for us." With a family, says Sherba, "I've learned to shift gears more quickly. I'm in my playing mode. Then I'm in my learning mode. I learn more quickly now. The more responsibility I have it seems the more I learn to divide myself better.

She has encountered some prejudice for being a mother and a musician. She doesn't believe she would have gotten a job she auditioned for in Atlanta if she had said she was pregnant. "People are willing to tell you what you can do even though only you can make that decision. I'm sensitive to people like that. This is my life. I take my kids with me. I do my job well. There is pressure to be either a mother or a musician. "She adds that America should become more progressive in its maternity leaves like many European countries.

"Balance is the key word. You have to have a certain flexibility. We travel with our kids. That's important to me. We won't leave them if that becomes a problem. I value our privacy and home life. We leave our job away from us when we are home with the children. But it's not just a 9 to 5 job; it's an important part of my life. I would play even if I didn't have the job. I'm still willing to do crazy things like a single person would, but the job has to be at a professional level."

"Are you a musician?" Judith Cavendish asked me when interviewed her. "If you were, you wouldn't have to ask me how I got into music. You either know it or you don't. This is what I was meant to do."

Cavendish, who teaches at the University of Charleston, is a Huntington native with two degrees from Marshall University. She has performed with the Charleston Symphony and the West Virginia Opera Theater. Her principal teachers were the late Jane Hobson of Marshall and Margaret Hoswell of the Manhattan School of Music.

In 1979 Cavendish made her national operatic debut with the Atlanta Lyric Opera. She has appeared in concerts across the United States and participated in the 1979 Aldeburgh Festival in Suffolk, England, at the invitation of Sir Peter Pears.

Cavendish advises young people, "Do your career first. Children should come after you are established. Stick to your goals." She also favors a solid musical education. "I've found too many people who do not have sufficient training in school. They miss the boat."

Cavendish's husband is a baritone and the two perform together. Because she once was married to someone who was not a musician and not interested in music, she now knows that "it's better if both are interested and share." Her children, ages 15 and 4, take care of each other sometimes. I also have an understanding mother who takes care of the children some, and my husband takes care of the children while I'm on tour. I juggle my career and family. It's tiring, but satisfying." Now that her son is older, she has begun traveling again for her career. "I'm taking up the reins again." She's returning to New York City where she will be auditioning and performing again.

Renay Conlin noted that she was interested in music from the time she first heard it on radio and television. People who liked her voice encouraged her to audition for Juilliard. Born in Manhattan and raised on Long Island, she is now a singer and piano player. She has performed with orchestras and operas and taught voice at Marshall University. She came to West Virginia when her husband took the job as conductor for the Charleston Symphony.

"We share a common interest," she said of her husband. "He plays piano for me at recitals. I can't imagine not being married to a musician."

Since the birth of her daughter eight years ago, Conlin has performed less frequently. "It's hard to juggle time. Opera takes so much time. Travel can be difficult." She takes her daughter along for some performances, and makes the most of practicing time while her daughter is in school.

Looking back, Conlin remembers an aunt who played piano and took her to operas. "Seeing a live performance was so important." Another influence was Joan Sutherland's record "The Art of the Prima Donna." "It was the most incredible thing I'd ever experienced, and I listened to it everyday."

Brenda Mullins, an organist, a singer and teacher, is also the first woman from West Virginia to play at the National Cathedral. An assistant professor at West Virginia State College and organist-choirmaster at St. John's Church in Charleston, Mullins got her bachelor's degree in organ performance from Oberlin College and her master's from Northwestern University. In addition, she had a year of study in Cologne, Germany as a Fulbright Scholar.

Although her husband is not a musician, he is supportive of her career, she says, and "attuned to the idea of women working. It's difficult to do all the things I do. The concept of a woman able to do all these things is by no means easy. I'm juggling it all, but Im not over-whelmed by it. I can fit everything in."

She recommends going to as many conferences as possible. Her favorite is the Westminister Choir College at Princeton. "It's well organized and presents the latest music in the field." Not going to conferences causes one, she says, "to lose contact with the rest of the world. I always think of myself as luckily split between academia and the church. I would recommend to younger musicians not to get into some program that is so rigid that it does not allow for personal growth. Otherwise they may grow to hate music."

Suzanne Riggio, Dean of the Charleston Conservatory of Music and Fine Arts, played French horn for the Charleston Symphony for twenty years. Now she manages musicians, keeps records for music groups, and does fund raising. She remembers cranking a gramophone and listening to Gershwin tunes as a child. Riggio wanted to join a band but could not until 1945, when the war was over because all the band directors had gone to war. One of her earliest instruments was so old she suspected it was made in the last century but her family could not afford a newer one. Later she managed to buy a newer one with the money she made working as a stringer for her local newspaper. She was paid by the inch, and she paid by the inch for her new trumpet.

She and her husband have five children. "It takes an inordinate amount of energy to combine work and family. My husband does some cooking and dish washing, and we have a maid to come in sometimes." Since he is also a musician, "we understand each other." They have even had simultaneous rehearsals in the house for different productions. But "It's exciting. We're doing what we like to do."

Riggio married when she was a college senior at Louisiana State University. Fifteen years and five children later, she finished her degree at West Virginia Tech. In the meantime, she had taken dozens of sessions at other universities.

As a woman musician, Riggio feels she has been judged by talent rather than gender. "I've always had leadership roles. I've hired orchestras for years. I'm in a position to feel the pulse of what is happening in the world of classical music."

An important book for her is *The Art of French Horn Playing*, by Philip Garkis, but she would like to write her own horn book. For years she has been collecting notes for it, and one day, when the time is right, she will write it.

Stephanie Pratt of Morgantown is a violinist who has chosen another career. With a master's degree in applied music from West Virginia University, she is a research assistant in the Office of Health Services Research at WVU and is doing graduate work in applied social science research. "This represents to me," she writes, "the beginning of a sort of emancipation from the violin. At the same time, I fear that I will have wasted all the years of work that made me into a professional caliber player. Is it enough that I am satisfied with what I have accomplished? Lately I am more certain that it is, and that I need to put the violin in perspective and move on.

"I still pursue orchestra and quartet freelancing and private teaching. I particularly enjoy my adult students, most of whom are professional women coming back to the violin after many years.

Judith Cavendish

"I have come to expect that I will play passages as flawlessly as I can, and sometimes find it difficult not to impose these standards on every performance I am involved in, especially when I am coaching young students or community groups. I occasionally even play in professional groups that demand little precision from the players. It's a challenge for me to play as well as I can under such circumstances.

"For me, the most discouraging aspect of being a violinist here is that there are so few fine players. Too often, I am the best player in a group. I learn, to a great degree, through observation, and playing in ensembles with more competent musicians motivates me. From a purely artistic point of view, it is painful for me to be involved in a sub-par performance of a work I love. Those are the times when I regret my decision not to pursue music more seriously. When I participate in a quality performance, the experience is all the more precious to me."

Pratt believes that viewing herself as violinist only caused her to postpone making a decision regarding a career. Furthermore, she says, "The time I have spent on the violin may have prevented me from doing other things that might have proven valuable. I never learned to sew well. I never learned to make a strudel. I haven't had a chance to read all of Doris Lessing's novels. I have rarely regretted my decision to continue playing the violin, though; nothing could have taken its place in my life, and I believe I am the better for it."

●

Be honest with yourself.
Assess how much you enjoy your music and how much talent you have.

—Consuela Sherba

Resources
Books

Ammer, Christine. *Unsung: A History of Women in American Music.* Westport, CT: Greenwood Press, 1980. Concise, well-researched survey of two centuries of women in American music; excellent bibliography.

Block, Adrienne Fried and Nuels-Bates, Carol, ed. *Women in American Music.* Westport, CT: Greenwood Press, 1979. This is a bibliography covering contributions of women in classical music; it contains more than 5000 entries.

Bowers, Jane and Judith Tick, editors. *Women Making Music: The Western Art Tradition, 1150-1950.* Urbana and Chicago: University of Illinois Press, 1986.

Cohen, Aaron. *International Encyclopedia of Women Composers,* Vol. I and II. New York: Bowker & Co.; 1981, 1982. These volumes offer the first comprehensive world history of women in music, and contain almost 5000 entries.

Cullinan, Elizabeth. *Yellow Roses,* New York: Viking, 1977. The short story "Dreaming" contained in this collection provides an insightful glimpse into the musical education of two sisters.

Green, Mildred Denby, *A Study of the Lives and Works of Five Black Women Composers in America.* Dissertation, University of Oklahoma, 1975.

LePage, Jane W. *Women Composers, Conductors, and Musicians of the Twentieth Century: Selected Biographies.* Metuchen, NJ: Scarecrow Press, 1980. This includes brief biographies of women in all areas of music, photographs, and reprints of reviews.

Merrill, E. Lindsey. *Mrs. H.H.A. Beach: Her Life and Music.* Dissertation, University of Rochester, Eastman School of Music, 1963.

Neuls-Bates, Carol. *Women in Music: An Anthology of Source Readings from the Middle Ages to the Present.* New York: Harper & Row, 1982.

Pool, Jeannie. *Up from the Footlights: Women Composers of Classical Music.* Boston, MA: G.K. Hall, 1981.

Redmon, Anne. *Music and Silence.* New York: Holt, Rinehart, and Winston, 1979. This powerful novel focuses on the stormy relationship between a talented woman cellist and a male teacher-mentor. The inner torment of a woman obsessed with playing music is beautifully drawn.

Skowronski, JoAnn. *Women in American Music: A Bibliography.* Metuchen, NJ: Scarecrow Press, 1978. Lists over 1300 books and articles, covers 1776-1976.

Tick, Judith. *Women Composers in the United States Before 1870.* Dissertation, City University of New York, 1978.

Zaimont, Judith Lang, ed. *The Musical Woman: An International Perspective 1983.* Westport, CT: Greenwood Press, 1983. The Musical Woman is a continuing publication that follows the achievements of women as entrepreneurs, critics, scholars, composers and conductors. Volumes include a "gazzette" section (which lists new recordings and published music, upcoming festivals and conferences, and awards and competitions), plus essays by individuals.

Periodicals

Ashley, Patricia, *"Discography of Women Composers," Ms.,* Nov. 1975.

Block, Adrienne Fried, "The Woman Musician on Campus: Hiring and Promotion Patterns," *High Fidelity/Musical America* 1975 Jun; Ma:22-23.

Boston Women's Music Newsletter, Box 91, Somerville, MA 01244. "Career Alternatives in Music: Some Advice from Outstanding Women Musicians," The Instrumentalist 1976 Dec. 31: 34+.

Heresies, P.O. Box 766, Canal Street Station, New York, NY 10013. Heresies #10: Women and Music is a collection of varied essays; it is available at the above address for $5.00.

Herrenkohl, Margaret, 1023 Stimel Drive, Concord, CA 94518. Ms. Herrenkohl has compiled an excellent collection of periodical articles concerning women in music. Available for $5.25.

Hinely, Mary Brown, "The Uphill Climb of Women in American Music: Performers and Teachers," *Music Educators Journal* 1984 Apr; 70(8): 31-35.

Hinely, Mary Brown, "The Uphill Climb of Women in American Music: Conductors and Composers," *Music Educators Journal* 1984 May; 70(9): 42-45.

Jepson, Barbara, "American Women in Conducting," *Feminist Art Journal* 1975/1976 Winter: 13-18.

Paid My Dues: Journal of Women & Music, Box 6517, Chicago, IL 60680. $8/4 issues.

Performance Opportunities, Sheet Music, and Recordings

Amateur Chamber Music Players, Inc., 633 E Street NW, Washington, DC 20004. This non-profit association supplies a directory to members every other year which lists names, addresses, telephone numbers, instruments played, and self-graded performance levels of members. Membership enables strangers to meet and arrange to play chamber music. Suggested annual contribution is $10.

American Women Composers, Inc., 6192 Oxon Hill Rd., Suite 406, Washington, DC 20021. Founded in 1976, this group helps women get works published, recorded, and performed. In addition, it is compiling recorded and printed materials for an archive of works by women. A quarterly newsletter is sent to members.

Arsis Press, 1719 Bay Street SE, Washington, DC 20003; (202) 544-4817; contact Clara L. Boone. Publishes works by women composers only; catalog is available.

Community Arts Orchestra, Division of Music, College of Creative Arts, West Virginia University, Morgantown, WV 26506; contact Margaret Lorince; (304) 293-4842. Composed mainly of adult community members and selected high school students, this group performs standard orchestral repertoire. Generally there are two concerts per year. String players are always welcome; wind players may need to audition. A low-key but rewarding opportunity to perform.

Da Capo Press, 233 Spring St., New York, NY 10013. The Women Composers Series is an ambitious printing of scores and parts of works by prominent women composers including Amy Beach, Cecile Chaminade, Clara Schumann, and Nadia Boulanger.

Kleeb's Piano and Organ. Mountaineer Mall, Morgantown. Offers workshops around the state for church organists.

Kschier Bros., Inc., 634 Washington Rd., Pittsburgh, PA 15228; (412) 561-2130. String instrument repair done promptly and well at a reasonable price. Violins, violas, and celli sold and rented — wide price range. Good selection of strings, resin, and supplies.

Music by Women Composers, Ohio State University, School of Music, 1866 College Rd., Columbus, OH 43210.

National Federation of Music Clubs Headquarters, Suite 1215, 600 South Michigan Ave., Chicago, IL 60605. A Directory of American Women Composers is available for $1.50. This lists compositions and publishing information for many women composers.

Northeastern Records, P.O. Box 116, Boston, MA 02117. Based at Northeastern University, this label offers hard-to-find recordings of works by Amy Beach, Fanny Mendelssohn Hensel, Rebecca Clarke, and others.

Roadwork, 1475 Harvard St. NW, Washington, DC 20009; (202) 234-9308; contact Amy Horowitz. Roadwork is a non-profit organization that does booking and promotion for performers in music, dance, and poetry.

The Romance of Women's Music. Pelican Records, P.O. Box 34732, Los Angeles, CA 90034. Nancy Fierro plays piano works of Clara Schumann, Cecile Chaminade, and others. Cost is $8.98.

Shar Products Co., 2465 S. Industrial Hwy., P.O. Box 1411, Ann Arbor, MI 48106; 1-800-521-0791. Shar offers a comprehensive selection of supplies for string players: strings, books about string playing, repair tools, bridges, resin, chin rests, and shoulder pads. String instruments, bows, and cases in varied price ranges may be requested on approval. Shar also carries a large selection of string solo and chamber music. Most items are shipped within 24 hours of receipt of order. All items except for sheet music are discounted.

Volkwein Bros., Inc., 117 Sandusky St., Pittsburgh, PA 15212; (412) 322-5100. Volkwein's carries a wide selection of all types of sheet music, and will accept mail and phone orders. This shop is also a good source for instrumental supplies, and maintains a large stock of student rental instruments.

Woman's Work. Gemini Hall Records, 808 West End Ave., New York, NY 10025. A set of recordings of works by women composers; includes 40-page booklet.

Women's Work. Performance scores by 15 contemporary women composers. Contact Anna Lockwood, Music Dept., Hunter College, 695 Park Ave., New York, NY 10021.

Traditional Appalachian Music:

The Strength of the Mountains, the Beauty of the Hills

Marianne Jahnke

Aunt Jenny Wilson

Michael Keller/WV Dept. of Culture and History

My acquaintance with traditional music dates only to my graduate school days when I shared a large, rambling house with a series of musicians, but my interest in music reaches back into childhood. I remember sitting at the piano trying to reach the pedals. In children's choir I began with the shortest robe and quit when the longest robe didn't quite reach my ankles. I sang in choruses, choirs, and madrigal groups through high school and most of college, until my scientific research took more and more of my spare time. So my credentials in traditional music make me an ardent consumer.

What is traditional music? When I started my investigation, I thought I knew. Traditional music is that great oral heritage passed along while one is felling trees or making dinner or poling or flatboating along the Ohio River or sitting on the front porch on a long summer's evening. This music rises to join the woodsmoke curling in the tops of the pine trees, the voices accompanied by fiddles, guitars, banjos, dulcimers, and the rhythmic thud of dancing feet. Folks who settled in various parts of the country sang different songs—all a reflection of the vast ethnic heritage and the daily experiences that tempered their lives. From these beginnings traditional music has evolved—bluegrass, country, Appalachian, blues and jazz styles, as well as songs of cowhands, railroaders, coal miners, field hands, and unions.

But through meeting women who make this music and through learning the art for myself, I found that traditional music represents more. This chapter is a personal odyssey that reflects my own interest and inclination as much as that of women I talked to or read about.

Traditional music is a dynamic experience—the translation of old-time melodies into living music that depends upon the combination of instruments that are playing together, the skill levels of the musicians, and the presence or absence of dancers.

As a beginning hammered dulcimer player, I learned that there are different "states" of playing—for oneself, with other musicians, and for an audience. Playing for myself is relaxation, experimentation, deepening the communication between myself and my instrument, myself and my fingers, myself and my music. Playing with others is excitement, challenge, turning familiar tunes inside out, inventing new variations within the framework of the melody because of the stimulation of other musicians playing other instruments. Performance before an audience is a one-way flow of music—from myself to the audience—which tightens my fingers on the hammers and speeds up my tempos to keep pace with my heart.

Another experience altogether is that of the square or contra dance. There are the musicians who are ready at a moment's notice to spill their music from their minds to their fingers, through their instruments to the dancers. Some dance tunes have their own accompanying dances, and the dance caller is expected to lead the dancers through a prescribed ritual of swings, allemands, right-and-lefts, and pass-throughs, or the dancers can do this themselves. Other dances can be done to any of several tunes. The music takes on a new dimension with a caller to talk through the moves of the dance and with the rhythmic thud and shuffle of the dancers' feet in time with the music, always with the music. "The music moves me through the dance, and my feet just follow," says Robin

Stewart, veteran square and contra dancer, and clogger. "Dancing with a good partner means added excitement. I can dance without ever breaking eye contact, and the resulting electricity really leaves me breathless. I love jazz dancing, rock 'n' roll and all that, but dancing with a good partner has its own kind of excitement."

The Uses of Traditional Song

Rhythm, excitement, pleasure, release—these are only part of the pull of traditional music. Traditional song has given a voice to women's stories as it has to the stories of the oppressed. Holly Tanner, a dulcimer player now living in California, explains what she found in folk music. "When started working with Frankie Armstrong in 1974, she turned me on to ballads as stories of women's lives—stories of women who were seduced and abandoned or who fought back and overcame their seducers or who were forced into arranged marriages, or who put on men's clothes to seek the adventure they could never have as daughters and wives" (Interview by Laura Soble in *Dulcimer Players News,* Summer 1984).

The Reel World String Band sings "She's a Coal Minin' Woman," a song which typifies the modern use of the traditional forms.

Jenny's husband left her with babies on her knee
He's long been gone, no money's come to feed her family.
Now miners make good wages in the county she comes from
And children do get hungry, Lord, and Jenny's back is strong.

She's a coal minin' woman, and that's what she wants to be.
She breathes that black and dusty air, wears pads upon her
    knees.
She's proud to be a woman and she's working to be free
To be a coal minin' woman and that's what she aims to be.

During the struggle to unionize the coal miners earlier in this century, the voices of women like Sarah Ogun Gunning were raised in song, fitting words of protest and outrage to melodies they had grown up singing. Woody Guthrie describes Gunnings's music in *Hard-Hitting Songs for Hard-Hit People.* "Sarah's homemade songs and speeches, made up from actual experience, are deadlier and stronger than rifle bullets, and have cut a wider swath than a machine gun could . . . She was so full of the union spirit that she found time to get out of the wind and rain and the hail of bullets from the deputies' guns, and make up her own songs and sing them to give nerve and backbone to the starving men that slaved in the coal mines."

Certainly, modern songwriters like Karen MacKay, Hazel Dickens and the members of the Reel World String Band show the influence of the traditional songs they sing so well. Regrettably, however, both Dickens and MacKay have had to leave their native West Virginia to make a living with their music.

Some of the Women of Appalachian Music

Patty Looman became involved in Appalachian music as a teenager, when she first heard the hammered dulcimer; then a relative gave her one just about the same time she learned about a great-uncle who had once built them. She and her mother began collecting the instruments.

Ethel Caffie Austin

Michael Keller/WV Dept. of Culture and History

Traditional song has given a voice to women's stories, as it has to the stories of the oppressed.

Looman is from Mannington, where dulcimer makers Russell Fluharty and Ralph Campbell still live and work, and where her mother, who ran a small business, was sometimes given musical instruments rather than cash in exchange for goods. Looman, who taught speech and drama in Michigan for several years, also taught dulcimer. Besides teaching, Looman and her mother have been presenting programs on the dulcimer for the last ten years in schools, nursing homes, churches, and many other places.

Why does she play? "For the joy of it," she says. "No other instrument has the tonal qualities of a hammered dulcimer. I can sit down at my instrument angry or tired or frustrated, and in ten minutes, that's all dropped away from me. Sometimes, when mother is watching television or entertaining a friend, I'll go in the next room and work out the fingering of a new song very quietly. It's so soothing."

Angel Chiango of Philadelphia has taught workshops for beginners in the hammered dulcimer at the Augusta Heritage workshop in Elkins. "I heard the records of hammered dulcimer playing and immediately decided that I had to learn," she recalls. "So I wrote to several folk magazines aroung the country to find out where I could learn to play. I took a course at Augusta several years ago, with John McCutcheon. In fact, took three years of courses there. Then I became an instructor."

Chiango performs with two bands, "Quilt" and "Heirloom," and founded a clogging group called "The Cobblestone Cloggers." She got her start as a professional in this way: "My clogging group went to audition for Busch Gardens, and we had to sit around and wait several hours. One of the other dancers was accompanied by a fiddler friend and she took out her fiddle and I took out my dulcimer. For a lark, we filled out an application as a group calling ourselves 'Heirloom.' Well, 'Heirloom' got the job, and the cloggers didn't! We had to tell them the fiddler was a full-time lawyer. They were willing to hire me alone, so played for two summers at Busch Gardens." Later the lawyer and guitarist who met at Augusta officially became "Heirloom."

Carrie Rizzetta of Valley Head is a partner with her husband Sam, a hammered dulcimer player as well as a builder and designer. Rizzetta, who left her job at the Library of Congress for the dulcimer business, says their business is based on his propensity to "build a new dulcimer for himself and sell his last dulcimer, one at a time. It's far from an ideal way to do business. Some of the instruments have a four-year waiting list." Rizzetta is limited by an injury from taking a large role in the building, but she is responsible for the business details.

Does she ever have difficulty in visiting the older musicians who might have old-fashioned attitudes toward women? "Frequently, when Sam and I go to visit with older musicians, the tendency is to send me off with the 'women-folk.' It just doesn't occur to them that I'm a musician, too."

Karen MacKay, formerly of Lewisburg, describes herself as a "singer/songwriter/performer and traditional instrumentalist" (she plays fiddle, banjo, guitar, dulcimer, and autoharp). She has been studying traditional music since age 14, and won her first contest at 15 at a local festival. She considers herself lucky to have been taught by some of the great old-timers, especially 83-year-old Aunt Jennie Wilson of Logan, to whom MacKay dedicated her first album, *West*

Virginia Woman. MacKay, at one time a worker with emtionally disturbed children, eventually made her music hobby her career.

"I'm on the road almost constantly—played festivals in nearly all fifty states—but these festivals are run for and by folks with very little money. My career comes first to me, and I've made that clear to my friends and my lovers. I don't ask anyone to travel with me. It's lovely when someone suggests it. Most of the time, though, I travel alone and mighty glad of it much of the time. I've learned to collect myself, to work, to write songs while driving. You can get a lot of work done on the road."

MacKay emphasizes the importance of promotion. But she insists on one difference. "I'm not going the traditional route of promoting myself. I've hired no agents, no talent agencies, no producers. I'm promoting myself by word of mouth, and my first record is on my own label, West Virginia Records."

Her second album, *Annie Oakley Rides Again*, appeared in 1984. But those who know MacKay are already fans of her first title song:

"I'm a West Virginia Woman, I'm the Appalachian Dream,
I'm the real mountain mama, just exactly what I seem.
I'm a hillbilly lady, I got country holler ways.
I'm a West Virginia Woman, West Virginia born and raised.
"I've got the strength of the mountains, the beauty of the
    hills."

How to Be Heard

Women in traditional music face the same problems other artists face in making a living. But, as many of them have discovered, it's hard to do it alone. Patty Loomis says of her earlier effort, "I made a record several years ago, and there's so much I've learned the hard way—because it never occurred to me to ask. I paid money to have the master cut, and a certain number of records made from the master, and I've gotten no money in royalties from any other copies cut from that master. I just trusted people and never thought to ask questions about contracts and things."

Others band together. Carol, dulcimer player with Queen Anne's Lace, a Pittsburgh-based group, says "We are making ourselves financially viable by several means. Sure, we play the dances, sell t-shirts, play music festivals. But we've gone beyond that by obtaining calendars of events published by several states (Pennsylvania, Ohio, West Virginia) and contacting the organizers of any festivals that might be interested in a band like ours. We're certainly not successful every time we make a phone call, but we've landed many jobs because of this aggressive approach." She adds, "We've been more active in promoting ourselves as a band because one of our members is in advertising—he got our t-shirts designed and has advertised us through channels that wouldn't occur to most traditional musicians."

The 1984 *Ladyslipper* catalog discusses the history of women in the music business and the problems faced by women in the music industry:

In 1974 the first National Women's Music Festival at the University of Illinois provided an opportunity for women musicians to hear, be heard, and learn from each other. The annual Michigan Womyn's Music Festival drew 8-10,000 participants in 1982, and is now a model

*You must be willing to take risks,
show an interest,
ask questions, take chances.*

—Angel Chiango

for other festivals. In 1978 women who distributed recorded women's music concerts created the Eastern Region Producer's Network.

Out of these beginnings have grown organizations such as Lady-slipper and West Virginia's own Artemis Sisters, a Morgantown based production company whose founders include Carla DeRuda, musician and teacher, and mail order services like Andy's Front Hall.

Andy Spence has become interested in the freelance production of concerts and festivals of traditional music. She is also the founder of Andy's Front Hall, a mail-order catalog business centered in Voorheesville, New York. Andy, married to Bill Spence, toured for several years with Fennings All-Star String Band where Bill played the hammered dulcimer and Andy called the dances. Arrival of daughter Hannah made traveling difficult and so began Andy's Front Hall.

Ten years ago, Front Hall Recordings released FHR-01 "The Hammered Dulcimer," and the company has now made 30 records, including its Back Porch series of instructional books and cassettes.

In addition they stock records, put out an annual catalog and have a mailing list of over 5,000 customers. "Hannah's grown up taking pennywhistles and records off the shelves of the Front Hall," Andy said in a telephone interview, "while we've avoided most of the hassles of two musicians married to each other, such as road tours and the absence from home life, and the single performer cared for (and sometimes supported) by a spouse at the expense of a second creative career."

Andy's Front Hall is one of the great resources of traditional and folk music. You can request almost anything in the field from her by phone and if she doesn't have it, she'll find out how to get it.

How to Get Started

First, come to dances, festivals, and workshops and watch and listen. It's very difficult to remain a bystander for long. I went to the Stonewall Jackson Heritage Arts and Crafts Jubilee and found myself sitting under the trees, watching several hammered dulcimer players. An older woman, Edna Epler, watched me for a time and finally said, "You want to play the dulcimer, don't you?" When I nodded, she called to her husband, Ray, who was playing softly on one of the dulcimers that he had built, and within a few minutes, I found myself seated in front of a dulcimer, having my first lesson. I have come to realize that this is the hallmark of traditional music—the welcoming of the stranger and beginner, the easy acceptance of the new musician with an instrument under arm, the "jam sessions" after dances and during festivals.

Angel Chiango says, "You must be willing to take risks, show an interest, ask questions, to take chances. You might be turned away, but you wouldn't get anywhere unless you tried. I learned clogging because at an Augusta festival I saw a man dancing in a pub, and I went up and asked, "What do you call this kind of dancing? How do you learn it?"

Kate Brett, a Morgantown banjo player and member of the local group The Worry Sisters, declares that she was interested in playing the banjo from the very first time she heard banjo playing on records. Kate is also a dancer who goes to many Pittsburgh area dances with her banjo and a bedroll in the back of her car—ready for late-night jam sessions afterwards.

Peggy Pings is a Morgantown area dancer, currently organizer for Friends of Old-Time Music's dances, who holds jam sessions at

Karen MacKay

Michael Keller/WV Dept. of Culture and History

I've learned to collect myself, to work, to write songs while driving. You can get a lot of work done on the road.

—*Karen MacKay*

73

irregular intervals on the front porch of her house in the country. These jam sessions are especially for beginners. In fact, she says, "If you can play more than ten tunes, you probably shouldn't come." In spite of several threats, her group (called The Kitchen Sink by the irreverent, after the only instrument not accepted) has yet to play for its first square dance.

If you live in the Morgantown area, investigate the Monongalia Arts Center, an organization increasingly committed to traditional music. It holds free or nearly free concerts throughout the year, offers classes with excellent instructors, and even has musicians playing during arts and crafts sales.

The Augusta Heritage Workshops in Elkins offer a variety of one-to-two week classes in many instruments at many skill levels. Musicians come from all over the country to take advantage of these courses.

Festivals

Augusta Heritage Festival: A five-week festival in Elkins, WV, at Davis and Elkins College. One and two-week classes in heritage arts and crafts are offered, including courses in autoharp, banjo, bluegrass, blues, Cajun dance, contra dance, fiddle, hammered dulcimer, lap dulcimer, harmonica, musical instrument construction, and stepdance week. The festival concerts, juried arts and crafts, dancing in the streets, all-night square dance, and gospel singing. Highly recommended.

10th Annual Smoky City Folk Festival: This three-day festival, in Pittsburgh, features square dancing, workshops all day Saturday, and an all-day free concert on Sunday. It is held at Carnegie-Mellon University and Schenley Park, both in Pittsburgh. For more information, contact Calliope House, 1414 Pennsylvania Avenue, Pittsburgh, PA 15233.

Coal Country Convention: This weekend festival, held in Mars, PA, includes a weekend of camping, dancing, and music. Workshops are given in clogging, square, and contra dancing, danceband musicianship, and fiddle and banjo playing. The festival is sponsored by Coal Country Conventions. For more information, contact Nancy Dwyer 5706 Darlington Avenue, Pittsburgh, PA 15217. Telephone (412) 321-4462.

Fiddlehead Music and Dance Week: This festival sponsors workshops in dance and music. In dance, contra, step-dancing, clogging, swing, square, jitterbug, two-step, and waltz workshops are given. In music, there are workshops in fiddle, danceband, rhythm and percussion, singing, piano, banjo, bass, and songwriting. In addition, there are sing-alongs, evening dances, and callers. For more information, contact Trina Royar, 1978 Old Annapolis Road, Annapolis, MD 21402. Telephone (301) 757-0774.

Stonewall Jackson Heritage Arts and Crafts Jubilee: This festival, held on Labor Day weekend, includes a juried craft show and competition in such areas as photography and fruit pie baking. Music is played throughout the festival and includes old-time, gospel, country, and bluegrass. Stage groups change approximately every 15 minutes, and musicians jam under the trees outside.

Winter Festival: This festival, held in mid-February at South Junior High School in Morgantown, generally includes 100 musicians form Maryland, Pennsylvania, and Ohio in addition to those from West Virginia. There is music on stage on Friday, Saturday, and Sunday, and there is a square dance on Saturday night.

Associations

Friends of Old Time Music: In the Morgantown area, this group meets monthly, generally on the third Saturday of the month, in the Mountainlair Blue Ballroom. For more information, contact Peggy Pings at (304) 291-8020.

Calliope House: One of Pittsburgh's many dance groups, this group meets monthly on the 4th Friday of the month, at the Third Presbyterian Church at 5th and Negley. For more information, contact Calliope House, 1414 Pennsylvania Avenue, Pittsburgh, PA 15233.

Elkins County Dance Society: The Dance Society offers a monthly dance series on the second Friday of the month on the campus of Davis and Elkins College, in Elkins, WV. The Dance Society also organizes several concerts a year. For more information, contact Mary Ladstatter at (304) 636-1800.

Newsletters, Catalogues, Clubs

Calliope House: Offers a schedule of concerts, square dancing, and folk dancing, all in the Pittsburgh area. Write: Calliope House, 1414 Pennsylvania Avenue, Pittsburgh, PA 15233.

The Dulcimist: A monthly, "The Dulcimist" contains a calendar of events, songs, interview, classified ads relating to traditional music, information about books, teachers, and accessories for the dulcimer (both hammered and fretted). Write: Phillip Mason, editor, P.O. Box 1052, Williamsburg, KY 40769.

Country Dance Bulletin: This bulletin covers dancers in several states and is especially helpful if you plan to be on vacation and want to catch local dances. Write: Editor, 6579 Allegheny Avenue, Tacome Park, MD 20912, or call (301) 270-3363.

Dulcimer Players News: This newsletter offers interview, music, reviews of recordings and books, and more. Write: Editor, P.O. Box 2164, Winchester, VA 22601.

Mountaineer Dulcimer Club: This club meets twice a year, in the Morgantown area, on the second Saturday in April and October for a day of jamming and performing on the dulcimer. Call: Patty Looman at (304) 328-2411.

Ladyslipper Catalog and Resource Guide: This catalog offers records and tapes made by women. The group is especially receptive to questions. Write: P.O. Box 3130, Durham, NC 27705. Or call: (919) 683-1570.

June Appal Recordings: One of many components of Appalshop, Inc., which also includes Roadside Theatre, Appalshop Films, Headwaters TV, Mountain Photography Workshop, and WMMF-FM, all dedicated to documenting and presenting the culture, traditions and social issues of people in the Appapachian mountains. For a free catalogue, write: June Appal Recordings, P.O. Box 743, Whitesburg, KY 41858. Or call: (606) 633-0108.

Andy's Front Hall: A great musician's resource, "Andy's Front Hall" offers records, tapes, books, musical instruments and accessories of all kinds. Whether you need a record or advice, write: Andy's Front Hall, Drawer A, Voorheesville, NY 12186. Or call: (516) 765-4193.

Photography:

I Can See Them in My Head

Nancy Abrams

Nancy Abrams

I'm always looking for pictures. I often find them as I'm driving and screech the car to a halt. But you have to be willing to stop the car and be late for wherever you're going. Sometimes my kids will be in the car screaming for me to hurry up or honking the horn, and I'll be trying to compose and shoot and hurry at the same time.

One time my six-year-old son asked me how pictures got from the camera to the paper. At first I tried to explain things like light, emulsion, silver, and all that. Finally, I paused and said it was mostly magic.

Soon after that I took him to work with me. I let him expose the print and put it into the Dektol. He held his breath as the image appeared, looked at me and said, "It *is* magic." Often to me, photography is magic, too. I told another woman photographer the other day, "We capture souls in silver."

The feminist "click" has literal meaning for West Virginia's women photographers. They are hooked on the medium.

"I call us the 'mole people,' " freelance photographer Mitzi Kellogg jokes. A former staff photographer for the Charleston *Gazette* and winner of many awards, Kellogg now shoots for herself. She calls photography "a man's market" in West Virginia because there are so few female photographers. "It's tough," she says of the conservative Charleston area. "There are so many photographers."

But a good photographer's work will stand out. "If you're a professional, if you've been a photographer for a while, your work will stand for itself." When she works for the clients, Kellogg says she "gives them what they want and more. Women photographers sometimes have to work harder."

Virginia Campbell of Sinks Grove still runs her own studio, at 70 years, though she has pared her work to part-time.

"I've just loved it all my life," she says. "My mother had one of the original Eastman folding cameras and I had one of the first 35mm's that ever came out."

Women, Campbell says, are "as good or better than men" in the photo business. "Women are better at weddings and portraits because of their rapport with their subjects."

Judith Walls agrees. She left an editing job at a monthly journal to enter a master of fine arts program in graphic design at West Virginia University. She has already had a one-woman show and is working on another.

"I find it surprising that most wedding photographers are men, and I believe women could do very well in this area. Probably the hardest area for women photographers is in some of the organized sports, where women have to overcome the old prejudices and assumptions they don't know anything about sports.

"I believe women can enjoy equal success in photography. Take heart from the example of Margaret Bourke-White, who earned a reputation in industrial photography, of all areas in 1928. She was *Fortune* magazine's first photographer and later a member of *Life*'s original staff."

Walls also concurs with Kellogg. "Expect that photography is often a physically demanding profession and that to succeed, you must strive to acquire a reputation as one of the best, and routinely produce work to maintain that reputation. Consistent quality and performance can overcome most barriers."

Laura Jones, a West Virginia native now living in Canada, has exhibited in over 50 one-woman and group shows across Canada and the U.S. Her photographs are included in three children's books and in over 100 other books and magazines.

In 1971, when darkrooms at the University of Toronto were for men only, Jones opened a darkroom for women. She has taught basic and advanced photography to women and arranged exhibitions of their work.

"It's hard work to establish oneself as a photographer," Jones says, "difficult for both women and men. I work very hard; I've cut out just about everything that doesn't relate directly to my photography or my family. Being a photographer means arranging one's life so that photography has a priority without neglecting one's family."

Professional photographer Barbara Sullivan likes to capture what Abrams calls magic. "One of the most gratifying aspects of photography is to capture a special moment in someone's life and show in the photo just what that person is feeling at that moment not just making a record of the mother and child or the newlyweds, but capturing what's going on between that mother and child, that couple.

Sullivan has been a professional photographer for 20 years. Her studio specializes in portraiture and special occasion photography such as weddings. "My father had a studio when I was a child, and he learned that if he wanted the darkroom door to stay closed, he had to let me in there first. I was fascinated by the work."

Marilyn Enslow, too, inherited a love of photography from a parent. But she at first denied that love.

"My mother was a professional photographer when I was a child and I was very jealous of photography. I vowed never to get into it myself. Then about five years ago my husband bought me a camera for my birthday, I enrolled in a photography class at Marshall University, and I absoutely blossomed."

Photography was just a hobby for Rebecca Johnson, assistant professor of journalism at Marshall University, "until I got into a darkroom and saw the 'magic water' work." Johnson teaches photography at Marshall and pursues an active freelance career. She "got into photography sort of by accident." While attempting to sell articles as a freelancer, she decided her work would have a better chance if she did some illustration.

Johnson claims a woman photographer's chances of succeeding in West Virginia are "whatever you want to create. In West Virginia, the opportunities aren't going to come out and slap you in the face." She adds that there is not that much work in the state—few newspapers, small cities—but adds, "Most people I know who stayed in West Virginia created their own little niche."

I won't take a picture unless the moon is right, to say nothing of the sunlight and shadow! Most of the time I have to be excruciatingly patient waiting for the light to get precisely right. Sometimes I have a tree cut down, have a stump removed, or a platform erected to get the proper perspective.
I have shot pictures from on top of boxcars and loaded trucks. If I'm in a city street, I often call the police to hold up or detour traffic while I photograph a place.

—Francis Benjamin Johnston,
quoted by Anna Shannon in
Missing Chapters

For those who seek publication, Johnson suggests they look at "small, special interest magazines." She also says it helps if they combine photography with reporting. If you have a hobby, she advises, so much the better. "Look for a publication in that area."

Mary Markey worked as a freelance photographer a couple of times, but was put off by "the insecurity of doing that for a living." She now works with photos as a historian. Markey is in charge of the photographs in the West Virginia Regional Collection at the West Virginia University Library.

Sullivan recommends that "if you're a serious amateur and want to better yourself in the mechanics of photography, take courses offered by art galleries, community colleges or universities. You have to become comfortable with the mechanics first, before you can deal with the aesthetics. To get good pictures, you can't be thinking about the camera settings. the camera must become such a part of you that the mechanics are no longer part of your thought processes. That frees you to think about the situation or person you're photographing.

Even after you've become a seasoned photographer, it's good to take a class once in a while. It forces you to use methods you don't use on a regular basis.

The most imporant things I've learned about photography have been from other photographers. This is a profession where people don't mind sharing what they know. Especially if you intend to get involved in photography and earn money, you should get together with other professionals. Join the Professional Photographers Association of West Virginia, for example. Twice a year they hold workshops, bringing in professionals who've really made it in photography and are well known for their work; it's so enlightening both technically and by giving you a sense of renewed enthusiasm."

Campbell agrees. When she attends a seminar, she says she "always picks up some new ideas." Campbell recommends that a serious principles—composition, color—can be valuable for anyone going into photography; beginners need education in that more than in the mechanics of a camera. The more education you have, the better a job you can do."

Other recommendations for the beginning professional: Francis Benjamin Johnston, a West Virginia native who was one of America's early female photographers, thought the qualities essential to a professional woman photographer—besides the courage to break with convention—were "good common sense, unlimited patience to carry her through endless failures, equally unlimited tact, good taste, a quick eye, a talent for detail, and a genius for hard work."

Both Kellog and Johnston stress the business aspect of photography. "You should know all the guidelines when you go into business," says Kellogg. "Know all the tax cuts. Small business seminars are good."

"If you have access to a computer, that's a great tool," notes Johnston. "Some knowledge of business, accounting and so forth is also helpful. The beginner needs to know how long will take a new business to get to the paying point so you have the capital to survive until then."

Although help from professionals—accountants, attorneys, etc., is nice, says Johnston, "you can quickly get involved with a bunch of professionals, go broke in the process and get confused in the end." She suggests the novice consult books before professionals.

*Always have your camera with you
and always have film.
Be willing to stop and shoot
and put everything else on hold.
I've risked my life
I don't know how many times—
I've put my car in the ditch—
to get unplanned pictures.
They're often the ones that
turn out to be my favorites.*

—Nancy Abrams

Dorothy Weatherford Busk of Canaan Valley entered photography as a second career. In partnership with her husband, she specializes in outdoor photography and still-life interiors. "Photography is difficult to get into if you're out in the hinterlands of West Virginia," Busk says. "It takes a certain amount of perseverance and dedication; you have to be a salesman.

"Teach yourself good record-keeping. It's not every artist's cup of tea, but it's critical. An accountant is a must, too, especially if you do a lot of traveling. It's useful to know what is tax deductible. Develop a good system of cataloging your work. Things accumulate so rapidly, and you need to be able to get to and sell what you have."

Busk says legal advice can be important. "Tricky things can happen with photography; you can ship work out to clients and never get it back, for example. We've learned that you should always have a signed contract. Get any business agreements in writing."

And I recommend that news photographers find out who owns the negatives they shoot, so when they leave the job, the negatives go with them.

Equipment

Although most of these photographers began with a single camera, often borrowed, most agree that two camera bodies are the minimum for any professional.

When Johnson's students seek her advice on purchasing a camera, she asks them first how serious they are about photography, and second, how much money they have to spend. If they're poor, she recommends the K1000 Pentax, but if there's no problem with money, she tells them "to go to a camera store and start picking up cameras. I say 'go feel the camera. If it works in your hands it's the best camera for you.'"

Johnson, and many professionals, prefer the Nikon system. Most also agree that if a novice starts with a good system, she can add equipment a piece at a time as the budget allows.

Markey started out with an Argus C3. "If it had had a light meter, I'd still be using it." She tells beginners, "Try to keep it as uncomplicated as possible and add equipment as you learn."

Walls, who works with WVU Photographic Services, shoots a wide variety of assignments. She says, "My essential equipment is two dependable camera bodies (so that I have backup and the capability of shooting both color and black-and-white or two types of film efficiently); at least one motor drive (particularly for action and wildlife work); a versatile collection of lenses and, possibly most essential for a photographer on the move, a camera bag that works for me.

Strong additions to the list are tough, protective lens shades, a filter system to cover your needs and one or two good, dependable bounce flash units. Always have a variety of film and lots of it, extra batteries and a good sturdy, versatile tripod."

Kellog advises people not to overload their camera bags. She prefers a monopod to a tripod and touts the use of clamp lights, which she always keeps in the trunk of her car. "I've learned to improvise," Kellog says. She says it's wise to keep sturdy, waterproof boots and a change of clothes in the car.

Sullivan says "for most on-site, mini-studio situations, a 2 1/4 inch format camera such as a Hasselblad is good. Also having a Mamiya twin-lens gives you the option back in the studio of printing vertical or horizontal. Other recommendations: a ladder and a background.

Recommended as basic equipment for on-location studio-type photography are a 400-watt-second light with either an umbrella or a soft box, a tripod, a hand-held strobe, an exposure meter, and a 100-foot extension cord.

I advise against buying the 50mm lens that most camera dealers try to sell with a basic camera body. Although they are more expensive, I recommend the beginner buy two lenses, a wide-angle and moderate telephoto. A zoom lens is a viable alternative, but many beginners find them difficult to focus.

Also, make sure your flash adjusts so you can bounce it off a ceiling or wall.

Sources of Supply

Most of the photographers interviewed use both local and mail order outlets for supplies. Campbell uses both but warns when she buys a piece of major equipment, "I like to buy from people who stand behind their stuff."

As a penny-conscious student, Walls has done a thorough job of investigating supply sources. Her recommendations: "For paper and film, I run price checks with the major suppliers in my area, ask specifically for bulk rates and quantity discounts which they may frequently be persuaded to give. With this information in hand, where I buy is determined by weighing price with availability from the suppliers in question and the time factor or deadline I may be facing.

I commonly deal with Superior and D-P Photographics in Morgantown, Kadet Photo, Wolk's and Photographic Supply in Pittsburgh. I have had help in color printing from Jan Cook's WV Color Lab in Kingwood (strictly prints from color negative film for professional photographers) and I also recomment Meisel for custom color printing. Their work is generally quality, and they are good about doing remakes if a problem arises.

For decent prints from average exposure slides, try the Slideprinter in Denver. Turnaround varies, but the rates are about the best I've seen. If you have a tricky slide that needs custom attention, however, you're better off to pay for custom work.

Addresses/additional information:

Meisel Commercial Photographic Services, 325 Great Southwest Parkway, Atlanta, GA 30336.

The Slideprinter, P.O. Box 9506, Denver, CO 80209.

WV Color Lab, Cook Building, 414 E. Main St., Kingwood, WV 26537, 329-1682.

Kadet Photo Supply Co., 1004 Fifth Ave., Pittsburgh, PA 15219.

Wolk's Kamera Exchange, 312 Forbes Ave., Pittsburgh, PA 15222, 412-281-2677 or 709 Liberty Ave., Clark Bldg., Pittsburgh, PA 15222, 412-765-0660.

The camera must become such a part of you that the mechanics are no longer part of your thought processes.

—Barbara Sullivan

Photographic Supply, 515 5th Ave., McKeesport, PA 15132, 800-245-6715.

Three others that I have not used, but are recommended by photographer friends who have:

Merrill Photographic Supply Co., 233 Hale St., Charleston, WV 25301.

Printers Products, Inc. at 632 8th St., Huntington, WV 25701, 722-2101: or 1114 Central Ave., Charleston, WV 25302, 344-3563.

VWR Scientific Inc., 147 Delta Drive, Pittsburgh, PA 15238, 412-782-4230 or toll free 800-242-3776.

Equipment purchases may be made from any of the above, as well as mail order specialty suppliers. I decide based on the item in question, as well as price. 'Gray market' suppliers such as 47th St. and others in New York City often do not give U.S. warranties. Sometimes this may matter; at other times it does not. Just be sure you know what you are ordering is what you really want, and if it is an item with little possibility of need for factory maintenance within a normal warranty period. I order from the cheapest *reliable* resource.

The larger houses such as 47th St., B & H Competitive Camera Corp. place regular ads in all of the photography magazines. Others of note are Porter's Camera Store, Inc., Box 628, Cedar Falls, Iowa 50613, 800-553-2001—which is great for all sorts of odds and ends; Spiratone for accessories—135-06 Northern Blvd., Flushing, N.Y. 11354-4063, 703-886-2000.and Doran Enterprises, 2779 South 34th St., Milwaukee, WI 53215 for limited darkroom supplies.

Darkrooms

The consensus is cleanliness is of utmost importance in a darkroom. Close behind, though, is adequate ventilation. "Years from now I still want those little hairs on my lungs," Kellog says. "A good ventilation system is a must. I don't care if your darkroom is a coat closet."

Other necessities, for Kellogg are an excellent enlarger (kept clean), one good safelights. "I'd like to know how many photographers have good eyesight after 20 years in a darkroomm and to a photographer, your eyes are everything.

If you take good care of your equipment, process carefully and properly, establish and stick to routine methods, you can avoid many of the accidents and omissions that are the bane of photographers. Have a checklist at hand if necessary. Establish an order in everything you do and a system for doing it and stick to it! This goes from how you pack your camera bag to how you maintain darkroom chemicals, to how you file and store negatives and slides, or mount and frame finished prints.

For example, keeping your dark room as clean and dust-free as possible can prevent a plethora of printing and associated problems. Using a different set of tongs for each tray in the printing process prevents contamination and prolongs the effective life of the chemicals. Repacking and handling your gear in a routine manner at each jobsite can prevent damage and loss of equipment."

"I try to keep people from buying cheap enlargers," says Johnson. She also stresses that every darkroom should have separate wet and dry areas which never meet.

Mitzi Kellogg: "The only way I can enjoy life is with my camera. I've become obsessed with it, I hope when I'm 90 years old I'll be shooting or somebody will ask me how to work a camera.

"Have the eye. It's all it takes . . ."

Judy Walls recommends *ICP Encyclopedia of Photography*, John Hedgecoe's *The Book of Photography* and *The Art of Color Photography*; Henry Horenstein's *Black & White Photography* and *Beyond Basic Photography*. "Photography 'picture' books are notoriously expensive, but most are well worth the investment if they have quality reproductions by major artists. Sometimes you can get publisher overstocks of great quality books at drastic reductions. And if you can't afford to buy them, at least leaf through them slowly!"

Walls believes the best, single resource is the new Ansel Adams Photography Series in three volumes: *The Camera*, *The Negative* and *The Print*.

Organizations

National Press Photographers Association. For press photographers only. P.O. Box 1146, Durham, N.C. 27702. Dues around $50/year. Includes subscription to monthly magazine and annual paperback *Photojournalism* series. Also entitles entry in Pictures of the Year competition and monthly clip contests.

Professional Photographers of West Virginia, Inc. c/o Executive Secretary Brenda Pavlik, P.O. Box 2539, Weirton, WV 26062, 304-723-2298.

Professional Photographers of West Virginia, Inc., (PPWV) is a trade association which promotes high standards of workmanship, and skill in professional photography.

There are several membership categories: active (at least 50 percent income from photography), associate (employee of an active member), affiliate (less than 50 percent income from photography), out-of-state, and a studio membership. Individual membership fees vary from $50 to $30, depending on membership category. There are about 115 members, including about a dozen from neighboring Kentucky, Pennsylvania, Virginia and Ohio.

A newsletter, *The Focal Point Flash*, is distributed monthly to all members. It allows members to advertise free for used equipment. The editor is J.T. Lawson, JT's Photography, 306 Little Oak Street, Williamson, WV 25661.

Professional Women Photographers, Inc., c/o Photographics Unlimited, 43 West 22nd Street, New York, NY 10010, 212-255-9678. Professional Women Photographers Inc., aims to promote intelligent appreciation of the best photographic art in general and the work of professional women photographers in particular. Membership is open to all photographers; most members are women, but men are welcome. Membership fee is $15 per year.

Professional Photographers of America, 1090 Executive Way, Des Plaines, IL 60018. 312-299-8161. An association for photographers in all levels of the profession, Professional Photographers of America caters to the entire photographic industry. Among its numerous functions are education, competitions, marketing, professional development, and business-related services.

There are 12 membership categories, ranging from fulltime studio owners and fulltime professional photographers to students of photography and retirees. Membership fees vary by category. At present, the annual membership fee for new members who enroll in the primary category—Professional/Active—is $95.

Society for Photgraphic Education, Women's Caucus, P.O. Box 1651—FDR Post Office, New York, NY 10150, 212-624-2365. The SPE Women's Caucus is a division of the Society for Photographic Education, an organization primarily for faculty in photographic education. Membership is open to everyone. Annual membership fee is $35. Special programming for women is scheduled by the organization's women's caucus during the 1985 national conference in mid-March.

Triangle, 441 State Street, Baden, PA 15005, 412-869-9281. An association of about 565 professional photographers of western Pennsylvania, northern West Virginia, and eastern Ohio, Triangle Professional Photographers Association provides continuing education and advancement of members' professional abilities, keeping them abreast of the latest in professional photography. Membership is open; annual membership fee is $30. In conjunction with the Community College of Beaver County, Triangle hosts the annual Triangle Institute of Professional Photography the second week of every January. According to Samual Pelaia, who coordinates the program, it is always a sell-out and brings 65-70 percent repeat participants. Credits earned at the Triangle institute apply toward the Professional Photographers of America's master's degree.

Suggested Reading

Books

Recollections: Ten Women of Photography, Margaretta K. Mitchell, NY: The Viking Press, 1979. Each distinguished photographer recollects her life and work. The ten are Berenice Abbott, Ruth Bernhard, Carlotta Corpron, Louise Dahl-Wolfe, Nell Dorr, Toni Frissell, Laura Gilpin, Lotte Jacobi, Consuelo Kanaga, Barbara Morgan.

Women in Photography: An Historical Survey, Margery Mann and Ann Noggle, San Francisco: San Francisco Museum of Art, 1975. Catalogue of exhibit by the same name that traveled nationwide from 1975-1976.

In/Sights: Self-Portraits by Women, Joyce Tenneson Cohen, compiler. Boston: Godine, 1978. 128 photographs by 68 photographers. Notes by the photographers. According to the October 1978 issue of *Ms* magazine, this book is "the first anthology of self-portraits by women photographers. It is the first attempt to show that women are really seeing, and what they are saying about what they see and experience, when they look at themselves throught the camera's eye."

Picture Palace, Paul Theroux. Fiction, Houghton-Mifflin, 1978.

On Photography, Susan Sontag, Dell, 1978. According to Terry Pervola, this is a book about how photography has affected everyone's vision and covers a general philosophy about the aesthetics of photography. She calls it a "powerful, sometimes distrubing book. For weeks I found myself looking at people as objects."

1985 Photgrapher's Market, Ed. Robert D. Lutz, Writer's Digest Books, Cincinnati, Ohio. According to Nancy Abrams, "if you're truly self-motivated and have the time and energy to freelance, *Photographer's Market* is a good how-to book on marketing photography."

Visual Impact in Print, Angus McDougall and Geral D. Hurley, Visual Impact, 1975. Abrams says, "As students, we called this the Bible of photojournalism."

Have the eye. It's all it takes . . .
—Mitzi Kellogg

Magazines and Newspapers

"The more pictures you see, the better photographer you're likely to become," says Abrams. She recommends *National Geographic* as "the ultimate photographer's magazine." She also recommends *Life* magazine. "The other news magazines often have good pictures, but they don't have the space to make their pictures big. I like my pictures BIG."

Camera Arts is "a very good magazine that is no longer published. It's worth looking up back issues at a public library."

American Photography gives "a good artistic and commercial overview."

Two publications by and for professional photographers: *Rangefinder* and the monthly magazine for members of *Professional Photographers of America.*

Modern Photography "can't be beat for the serious amateur."

Abrams recommends both Charleston, WV, newspapers as "excellent photo newspapers."

Modern Photography and *Peterson's Photographic* provide good technical tips.

American Photographer provides good quality technical advice, but one photographer we interviewed complained that that magazine has far too much sexist imagery, prompting frequent angry letters to the editor by women photographers.

One novice photographer pointed out that the camera companies, such as Nikon, frequently have excellent magazines.

Writing:

Breaking Through the Boundaries

Linda Yoder

Devon McNamara

"To say 'I am a writer' was a hurdle for me because I always wanted the word 'good' to be in that declaration," says Susan Williams, who writes for the Charleston *Gazette*. "Fear that the word 'lousy' would more easily fit kept me from claiming my title. But over the years I crept up on feeling comfortable saying, 'I am a writer.'

"I was about to pull the chain on the lamp by my bed and go to sleep when for some inexplicable reason this thought ran through my head: I paid for this lamp with my writing. It's a wonderful hand-made lamp created by a woman potter whose work like and collect. For the last three years, I've supported myself completely on my writing, but it never struck me until the other night. I might say the light dawned on me when I was about to turn it off."

Like Williams, many approach the title of writer with diffidence; others, like Barbara Smith of Philippi, author of *Six Miles Out*, claim it with joy. "I am, in the nooks and crannies of time, a writer. Actually, I write constantly—probably an average of six or seven hours a day, maybe four or five. Most of it, though, is administrative and technical writing.

"I can't *not* write.

"Writing for me is not a separable activity. It is a part of the whole. I can't not write, but I also can't not run and play golf and teach and love my kids and laugh with my friends and read and knit and plant flowers and wash cars. And all of it, I hope, is an act of worship."

Poet Llewellyn McKernan of Huntington has a simple explanation of why she writes: "Although I've written other things—short stories, translations, newspaper and magazine articles—I'm really a poet, and recently was asked to tell a class of creative writers how I became one.

"I'm a poet because as a child I could not go to sleep at night. I would lie awake for long moments in a blue twilight where my imagination, using my eyelids for a screen, would swing me from one softly lit scene to another, merging reality with dream so wondrously I never wanted to leave. As an adult the closest I come to getting back to that pristine state of innocence is when I put pen to paper to write a poem: experience a bird, my words a cage where sometimes it sings."

Getting Started

Kathleen Diehl, most recently a writing teacher at Potomac State College, is used to answering the question of getting started. "I have met many people who have a burning desire to become a writer, but they don't know how to go about it. Many of them have been talented, and others are kidding themselves.

NOONTIME EXPERIMENT
Grey sky, orange zinnas.
I want them in my poem.

                    —*Mary Lucille DeBerry*

"The first thing I tell them is that it is one of the most difficult things they will ever do. It takes a great deal of time, it is frustrating, it isn't fair how writers are treated when they try to publish, it is lonely, and other writers can offer little sympathy because they are having problems of their own."

Diehl insists upon three things: "First, I don't think you can be a writer unless you are well read. That means reading all the classics, searching out the well written books from the last forty years, and always searching for more. Look at best selling books with a critical eye, trying to separate the ones that may go on to become classics. There aren't a lot. I stress looking for good books from other countries, as the U.S. doesn't have the handle on well written books; we are way down on that list.

"Second, you must learn how to critique. You have to know what made that classic last, why something is handed an award. Learning this, I feel, is nothing short of fun. When you start analyzing a book or short story, and discover for yourself all these wonderful techniques, wonderful passages, turns of phrases, metaphors, you feel reborn. But you can't discover these things until you know the foundations."

Diehl's third point is, of course, to write. "Every day you have to sit down at the typewriter or notepad, and even if you write gibberish, you have to do that. One of the best pieces of advice I've ever received was from a teacher who told me I was a good writer, first, then said, 'However, you have to write a hundred things before you get one that is publishable.' After I got over my shock at this, he added: 'You better go write number one tonight, number two tomorrow. The sooner you start, the sooner you'll get to a hundred.'

"Actually, I didn't get to a hundred, but I did write about sixty pieces before I got my first one published. By then, I had started to develop a style of my own, and I had got some of the garbage out of my head. When I look back, now, on those first pieces, they were important to me then, but the stuff I am writing now comes from below the surface that they came from from a place I didn't know I had when I first started writing. My technique gets better and better too, so all that studying and all that writing and all those rejects were my dues. I paid them, so to speak, even though I feel they are on-going. I still don't get every single thing published, but I understand the system better, and know that every day is a chance to do something new."

How did I get started? Leah Richards, who teaches writing at Alderson-Broaddus College, answers, "My writing really began with a need to try to convice fellow teachers that they could do a better job. Fortunately, I then fell under the influence of one of the best composition theorists today—Janet Emig—when I attended a summer workshop at the University of Chicago on "Teaching Writing as an Art and a Science." There I had my confidence built and developed an understanding of what real writing is—an involvement with personal experience. I learned that writing is a way of clarifying what we know but don't realize we know, and as we clarify it for ourselves, we make sense for others—sometimes. Here, also, I learned the value of the workshop situation when I was told where I had failed to say what I had thought I had said, or when something trivial to me made an impact on others. As a result, I turned to poetry where I could resort to figurative language and brevity in saying something I was in the process of learning."

So many things go into the making of a writer. Jayne Anne Phillips, author of *Machine Dreams*, tried to deal with this question in an interview for *Vogue*, July, 1984. "I don't think writers teach themselves how to write. It's an outgrowth of personality. Isolation. Secrecy. Especially for women. When I started to write, there was a feeling of absolute privacy. It may have had to do with shyness. With risk. Most people who write don't have much choice. A writer is a very alone person who tries to break through the boundaries of what is her own personality. I never decided to be a writer. I just ended up one."

Beginning Again

Some of the most poignant stories about getting started in writing have come from women who either got started quite late in life or were forced by circumstances to put writing aside. Three Morgantown poets—Georgia Heaster, Betty Donley Harris, and Edith Love shared such stories. Betty spoke for the others when she said, "I do not write for a living, but I write in order to live." Betty and Edith both remarked upon the need for attention in painful circumstances, because poetry might come out of it, remindful of poet Susan Griffin's warning to "stay with the experience, because this experience renders a precise meaning." (Harris tells her own story in "I Write in Order to Live.")

Patricia Dobler, a Pittsburgh poet who returned to poetry after her children were grown, found that the experience bordered on the miraculous. "I was raising children and working from the time I was 22 until just about eight years ago, when my kids needed me less and my own need, that is, to return to poetry, became impossible to ignore. I was working as a secretary in El Paso, Texas, when writer Raymond Carver encouraged me to take his workshop in poetry. I was really scared about whether or not I could still put anything on paper—I had written in college, won some college prizes, had been accepted into the Iowa Workshop but did not go—my life had taken such steps away from poetry. I loved it, loved it desperately but was so frightened.

"We moved to Pittsburgh and I graduated from the MFA program at the University of Pittsburgh. My new book, *Talking to Strangers*, will be published this year from the University of Wisconsin Press.

"Every bit of this is a miracle to me. I do not know why I was suddenly permitted to write poems again; and I mean this absolutely, for that is how it feels: I was given permission to do my work. In part, it was the lessening of household pressures; my husband consistently supported my tentative efforts to get back to work; and I had great teachers; but honestly, the way it feels is this: for years my life was such that I could not write and then, suddenly, it was like a curse being lifted or as if I had emerged from under the lake.

"I know of many other women writers who were able successfully to combine family life with work life. I was not able to do this, in part because of economic necessity. But I don't know of a single woman writer with children who hasn't had grave difficulties balancing her life."

A discussion with her husband finally gave her courage to begin again, Dobler says. "I was expressing my terror at returning to poems and probably failing. He said, 'You must *take* the time and space you need. No one will give it to you. The kids and I, too, will take everything

The stuff I am writing now comes from below the surface from a place I didn't know I had when I first started writing.

—Kathleen Diehl

you're willing to do for us, but if you want this for yourself, you have to reach out your hand and take it.'

"And you know, for women of my generation, that is a hard thing to do, to *demand* your time and space. I was amazed at how easily the family adjusted itself to my new life."

Penna Drew of Pittsburgh came to poetry after a career in medicine. "All through my professional years I had continued to write, but everything simply went into a file drawer except what was written for medical journals. Then I saw retirement ahead of me, and I decided that I had better get going if I really meant to write. And if I was to get going, I must have some feedback. So I applied to, and was accepted into, a Master of Fine Arts program, knowing that there would be no hiding place down there. Stuff would have to be put on the table, exposed, and ripped apart.

"Without question, the MFA program has been a boon beyond words. Even at its most tiresome moments, I would recommend some such open criticism to anyone. At first I thought every critique must be God's word; I obediently changed poems and paragraphs to suit the tastes of the other students. Then one day I realized that, like medical students, some of them simply had to be heard talking (whether it made sense or no), that they had no real sense of responsibility to me—so I fought back."

Keeping it Going

Writers talked about the nitty-gritty of a writing woman's life. How do they make time to work? How do they manage the care of children, care of home, the earning of a living? What about work space, about equipment, about resources? What about the business of being a writer—about agents, taxes, and the law?

Bonni V. McKeown of Capon, author of *Peaceful Patriot*, writes, "Since the birth of my daughter in 1982 I have produced almost no 'creative' writing. All of my writing skill has gone into my extended family's business; all my creativity has gone into surviving in the 'real' world. But my observation eye has kept open the whole time, and the more life I live, the more I will have to say when I do start writing again. I don't feel blocked or deadened; rather, my creativity has gone into other channels and will resurface as writing.

"Alice Walker's article in *Ms.*, 'One Child of One's Own,' is pretty much true for me. My daughter has opened new worlds to me while taking an awful lot of time and energy. I would think that other children would take more of those without a corresponding increase in insight."

Says Amy Jo Zook, a Mechanicsburg, Ohio, poet, "I had trouble with my writing when my kids were small. It was so interrupted that I largely put writing aside and painted instead. But my kids do understand about writing. . . . Teaching and going to school do not slow down my writing; in fact, they generally increase its tempo, unless I get too bogged down in writing papers for class."

Workplaces vary—from the "two card tables in my husband's office" of Esther Corderman, author of *Echo from Rose Hill*, to Zook's enviable spread: "I work most seriously in a study which we very carefully planned for that purpose. It has floor-to-ceiling bookshelves on three walls, and the windowed wall has my music, stereo, records, tapes, and plants sitting and hanging in front of the two large uncurtained windows. I have a typewriter always before me, a HUGE desk,

And you know, for women of my generation, that is a hard thing to do, to demand your time and space. I was amazed at how easily the family adjusted itself.

—Patricia Dobler

dictionaries and other necessary books just behind me, and all my notebooks and paper, also all my published work just at my fingertips, in case I need to check something already in print." Morgantown writer Barbara Rasmussen confesses, "I have a wonderful attic studio that is almost womblike in its kindness to me, but everyone else in the house likes it too, so often I have a lot of company."

Richards writes: "Work space: alone. Comfortable chair and footstool to prop my legal pad on my knees. Pleasant view of nature. [Here she pencilled in 'I just saw two deer.'] Rough drafts are always by hand."

Barbara Smith responds, "As for work space—ha! I have to write wherever and whenever the cracks open for a moment. The space and the equipment therefore depend upon wherever I am at the moment. I can and do use a word processor, but that's usually after beginnings or first drafts. Usually, because of the time and space factors, the first shot is fired by hand—on any kind of a scrap of paper with anything that leaves a mark.

"Time? Like now—very, very early in the morning or like yesterday—in the middle of an afternoon meeting—or like the day before—in the dentist's office—whenever and wherever."

Drew discovered maids' rooms in the apartment building where she lives, a building "left over from the elegance of the twenties," rented one of them, and now, without putting on boots or a coat, descends into her phoneless cell. "One window provides me with piece of tree and a deserted bird's nest. There are prints on the walls (bare walls would be too much asceticism). Piles of paper proliferate when I'm not looking. The only equipment is my p.c. which I had to learn to ride while it bucked and I swore. It's now absolutely essential because of the ease of erasure and revision. Without question I consider my space ideal."

About word processors writers were rarely neutral. Bonni McKeown: "The least in obstacles between my head, my fingers and the paper, the better." Others see the machine as a way to eliminate the obstacles.

Meredith Sue Willis writes: "It is changing my work in all kinds of subtle ways that I try to be aware of. One big change is that I have to keep my coffee ten feet away from me. Another is that my hands can almost keep up with my mind, and one result is that little chatty phrases that I must have edited out subconsciously in the old days (not wanting to type more than necessary) are now showing up on the little green screen. On the other hand, I polish more and with greater ease. I also have a semi-mystical sense that before I have printed something out, when it is still on disk only, that it is unborn, in my mind, rich with all the possibilities of a completely fresh idea."

Writers almost overwhelmed me with "favorite books;" they were passionate about some. The two most often mentioned were Tillie Olsen's *Silences* and Janet Sternburg's collection of essays by writers, *The Writer on Her Work*. Several mentioned, surprisingly, *Georgia O'Keeffe*. One of these was Willis, who goes on to describe it as "a coffee table book of paintings by the great American painter with her comments. The text is spare—a ninety-year-old's summary of life—and the pictures are wonderful. It is a true text of what it means to live as an artist. I am also, I must confess, a sucker for any biography of any woman writer, especially old ones; life stories of George Eliot,

I have a semi-mystical sense that before I have printed something out, when it is still on disk only, that it is unborn, in my mind, rich with all the possibilities of a completely fresh idea.

—Meredith Sue Willis

Andrew Weinberger

Meredith Sue Willis

George Sand, Charlotte Bronte, and Virginia Woolf rarely get past me. I also go for lives of Marilyn Monroe and Judy Garland and Loretta Lynn." McKernan's favorite is Colette's *Earthly Paradise: An Autobiography*, drawn by Robert Phelps from her writings because "Colette makes her life a work of art and art her life's work."

Mary Lucille DeBerry of Morgantown cited Eudora Welty's biography with its West Virginia background (*One Writer's Beginnings*) and Agnes Smith's essays: *Speaking as a Writer*, available from Westwind Press, Rt. 1, Box 208, Farmington, WV 26571. Williams answered, "Everything Virginia Woolf ever wrote and *Out of Africa* by Isak Dineson." Among Diehl's favorites are Anais Nin's *The Novel of the Future*, Flannery O'Connor's *Mystery and Manners* and *The Habit of Being*, and Eudora Welty's *The Eye of the Story*. Maggie Anderson finds these, among others, essential: Dorothea Brande's *Becoming a Writer*, Sylvia Plath's *Letters Home*, and Anne Truitt's *Daybook* (*The Journal of an Artist*).

Geting It Out

Some writers, such as Corderman, take the plunge and publish their own works. "After many rejections of my first novel, a publisher agreed to take it if I would allow cutting. I did not realize the magnitude of the cuts until the work was on the market; it no longer conveyed the message of the original." Nor did the publisher promote the work adequately. After that, printing and marketing her second novel, *Echo from Rose Hill*, was a much more rewarding experience.

At a GoldenRod Writers Conference in Morgantown, Smith discussed the "glory and gloom" of writing in West Virginia. First, there is the difficulty of getting published. There are precious few Appalachian publishers, fewer West Virginia publishers. The standard reference work *Literary Marketplace* lists no publishers at all in West Virginia. Publishers outside Appalachia are not particularly interested in Appalachian work. Or, if they have published such a work, say "We already published one . . ." The second difficulty, that of isolation, is related.

Free-lance writer Rasmussen is concerned about a subtle and peculiar form of discrimination, that is, expectations about what an Appalachian, especially West Virginian, return address should mean. She remarks about an article written by "an enthusiastic Washington D.C. government worker who was hard at work restoring her run-down West Virginia hideway," who "pondered such issues as chewing tobacco, strip mine justice, mules and hillbillies—barefoot and pregnant, of course." In contrast to that absurdity, she cites an article of her own, written on a speculation assignment for a well-known magazine, but rejected, as the editor wrote, although 'clear and strong,' for lack of 'deft personal touches.' I am beginning to fear, Rasmussen continues, "that there are certain expectations about women writers in Appalachia, and those do not include well-written pieces on matters of wide public interest." She is particularly concerned that while women writers in Appalachia are fighting battles for a better deal, their writing will reinforce stereotypes about their region.

Other effects of the Appalachian landscape upon women's writing are more subtle. In "A Great Tug at the Heart," (*Trellis 3*, Summer 1979) Anderson, McKinney, and Phillips discuss the effect of connectedness with this landscape and the objects that accumulate in it. All three women were in the process of moving from one home to another at the time the conversation occurred; all three felt the need to remark upon the "long record of family connections" and the way these connections—and the natural material objects that embody them—persist in the writing.

Getting Together

Writing is a solitary occupation. Yet writers need each other, need to share, to read aloud, to criticize, to laugh together. These things happen at writing workshops. Morgantown writer Gail Adams compares two of them: one, a week-long session at Duke University, where formal application was made and fees were high; the other, a low-cost, women-only (although not by intention) group at WildAcres Conference Center in North Carolina.

"At Durham," she writes, "the schedule was rigorous. Work which had been submitted and critiqued in advance was made available to each writer and discussed. D.M. Thomas was an excellent teacher; he not only paid attention to the participant's work but also read from his own and others' works. There was often an in-class writing exercise devised to make us think about working with words. A break for lunch, a brief rest and recuperation time in the early afternoon, and then the small afternoon workshops began. Evenings were dedicated to dinner, readings by well-known writers, and then wine and cheese and talk about writing with the visiting reader/author.

"There was no time scheduled for the participants to read their own work, nor was there much time for writing, since the reading load was tremendous. However, this was wonderful for me and just the kind of stimulation I needed. I stayed up late every night reading and writing and enjoying a life so different from the one I'd left. Most valuable for me was the encouragement and support I received from both workshop writers and teachers concerning my work. I now correspond with two of my teachers and don't hesitate to ask them questions about my work.

"The second workshop was again for a week. We gathered at Wild-Acres Conference Center, which provided a serene and gorgeous setting. This meeting had about it elements of slumber parties, consciousness-raising sessions and hard writing workshops, in addition to good times and silly fun. Here I learned the best stuff about agents and word processors and portable typewriters and how other women were organizing their daily lives and their writing. Much was shared here that would have been impossible in the more academic/professional atmosphere at Duke. Almost everyone brought useful information along—journals and guidelines and directories and places to submit and contest information, anything that could be helpful to writers. The level here varied tremendously from very professional, making money off writing, to just beginning, but the group was a wonderful meld.

"Both weeks provided me with what I most needed when I needed it: Duke with the affirmation that I was not foolish to take my writing seriously and that I should pursue it, and WildAcres with support and encouragement and the acknowledgement that it takes a long time, and that others share this struggle and even have fun while they're doing it."

Writing is a solitary occupation. Yet writers need each other, need to share, to read aloud, to criticize, to laugh together.

Resources

Poets and Writers, Inc., 201 West 54 Street, New York, NY 10019. 212/757-1766. A wealth of resources here, including an excellent newsletter, *CODA,* a directory of writers, and a "Sponsors List," a list of organizations sponsoring programs for writers.

West Virginia Writers, Inc. President Joyce Stover, P.O. Box 138, Kenna, WV 25248. The organization has many active local chapters. A former president, Jack Zierold, says that membership is open to residents of West Virginia who have "any kind of interest whatsoever in the written word, even merely as readers. Readers, we find, know more about writing and writers than most writers." WVW, Inc., sponsors an annual awards program. People from any state are welcome at the workshops and conferences and may subscribe to the quarterly newsletter.

Since the birth of my daughter I have produced almost no "creative" writing. But my observation eye has kept open the whole time, and the more life I live, the more I will have to say when I do start writing.

—Bonni McKeown

West Virginia Poetry Society, Calvert Estill, President, One Morris Street, Apt. 707, Charleston, WV 25301.

A Writer's Work, 1622 Kenwood Road, Charleston, WV 25314, offers workshops, consulting, and editorial services. A Writer's Work is the enterprise of Faith Holsaert, who also gives readings from her own fiction.

Feminist Writers' Guild, P.O. Box 9396, Berkeley, CA 94709. Has regional chapters.

International Women's Writing Guild, P.O. Box 810, Gracie Station, New York, NY 10028.

Marshall University's Birke Writers Series. Brings well-known writers to campus. Contact the English Department, Marshall University, Huntington, WV 25701.

FREEHAND, INC., P.O. Box 806A, Provincetown, MA 02657. A learning community of women writers and photographers. "We seek students who begin with a love of their work and a belief that the creative power in each of us goes into the work and strengthens all."

Fear of Filing: A Beginner's Handbook on Record Keeping and Federal Taxes for Performers, Visual Artists and Writers. Supplements prepared annually. Volunteer Lawyers for the Arts, 1560 Broadway, Suite 711, New York, NY 10036.

Grants and Awards Available to American Writers. PEN, 47 Fifth Avenue, New York, NY 10003.

Guide to Independent Study Through Correspondence Instruction. A Peterson's Guide. Available for $4.50 plus $1.25 postage through NUEA Book Order Department, P.O. Box 978, Edison, NJ 08817. Lists both credit and non-credit courses. Kathleen Diehl suggests, "These are good to send manuscripts when you have nobody you trust to read them and give you an honest evaluation. They don't cost very much, and you can bounce several manuscripts off the instructors which makes the courses worth their cost. Especially helpful if you lack the confidence to know whether or not something is ready for publication."

Literary Markets. 4340 Coldfall Road, Richmond, B.C. V7C 1P8. *LM* has published a list of 50 feminist poetry/fiction markets which can be ordered for $2.00.

Bring Out Your Own Book. Barbara McFadyen and Marilyn Gayle. Godiva Publishing, Box 42305, Portland, OR 97242.

Guide to Women's Publishing. Polly Joan and Andrea Chesman. Dustbooks, Box 100, Paradise, CA 95969, 2nd. edition, 1981. Lists many women's presses and periodicals, and describes their history, philosophy, and what they publish.

The Writing Business, A Poets and Writers Handbook. By the editors of *Coda: Poets and Writers Newsletter.* How to deal with the business of being a writer — from manuscripts to contracts to taxes. Pushcart Press, 500 Fifth Avenue, New York, New York 10110, 1985.

"On Giving Readings — A Checklist for Writers." Nitty-gritty advice from well-known poets. Send $1.00 and SASE to Poets and Writers, Inc., 201 West 54th Street, New York, NY 10019.

"Helping Writers Help Themselves." A list of groups that offer information and services to writers, including awards and publications. Send $1.00 and SASE to Poets and Writers, Inc., 201 West 54th Street, New York, NY 10019.

"On Cloud Nine: 24 Heavens for Writers." A list of writers' residences and colonies. Send $1.00 and SASE to Poets and Writers, Inc. 201 West 54th Street, New York, NY 10019.

"A Writer's Guide to Federal Income Taxes." Tells how the tax system applies to writers, and how to manage it efficiently. Send $1.00 and SASE to Poets and Writers, Inc., 201 West 54th Street, New York, NY 10019.

Personal Fiction Writing. A guide to writing from real life for teachers, students and writers. Meredith Sue Willis. Teachers and Writers Collaborative, 5 Union Square West, New York, New York 10003.

The Publish-It-Yourself Handbook. Literary Tradition and How-To. Bill Henderson, Editor. Pushcart Press Revised Edition, 1980.

Write On, Woman. Lynne D. Shapiro, publisher and editor. 345 West 87 St., New York, NY 10024. A writer's and artist's guide to women's alternate press periodicals.

The Writer on Her Work: Contemporary Writers Reflect on Their Art and Situation. Janet Sternburg, ed. New York: Norton, 1980. *Many* area writers responded citing this book as a tremendous resource.

Writer's Market. Writer's Digest Books, 9933 Alliance Road, Cincinnati, OH 45242. Published annually, this provides information on the magazine market.

Some Regional Publishers and Publications

Hill and Valley, Shirley Young Campbell, Editor. 4512 Lancaster Avenue, Charleston, WV 25304.

Grab a Nickel, Barbara Smith, Editor. Barbour County Writers' Workshop, c/o Alderson-Broaddus College, Philippi, WV 26416.

Goldenseal. A quarterly magazine devoted to traditional life of West Virginia. Ken Sullivan, Editor, Department of Culture and History, The Cultural Center, Capitol Complex, Charleston, WV 25305.

Gambit, Jane Somerville, Editor. Parkersburg Community College, Parkersburg, WV.

Laurel Review, Mark DeFoe, Editor. Department of English, West Virginia Wesleyan College, Buckhannon, WV 26201.

Three Rivers Poetry Journal, University of Pittsburgh, Pittsburgh, PA 15260.

Wind Magazine. Route 1, Box 809, Pikeville, KY 41501.

Mountain State Press. c/o The University of Charleston, 2300 MacCorkle Avenue, SE, Charleston, WV 25304. Has writing competitions.

Seneca Books, Daryush Farudi, Rt. 6, Box 81B, Morgantown, WV 26505. 304-594-1324.

University Editions, Ira Herman, Publisher (incorporating Aegina Press), 4937 Humphrey Road, Huntington, WV 25704.

Back Fork Books, Merle Moore, Publisher. Back Fork Books, Inc., Drawer 752, Webster Springs, WV 26288.

Jalamap Publications, 833 Scenic Drive, Charleston, WV 25311.

McClain Printing Co., 212 Main Street, Parsons, WV 26287.

West Virginia University Press, WVU, Morgantown, WV 23606.

Conferences and Workshops

West Virginia

GoldenRod Writers. In care of George Lies, 525 Grove Street, Morgantown, WV 26505.

Barbour County Writers' Workshop. In care of Barbara Smith, Alderson-Broaddus College, Philippi, WV 26401.

West Virginia Writers. In care of Joyce Stover, P.O. Box 138, Kenna, WV 25248.

Virginia

University of Virginia-SW Center Creative Writing Workshop. Rachel Fowlkes, Director, 100 Court Street, Abingdon, VA 24210.

Virginia Highlands Festival Creative Writing Day. Elen Shupe, Chairperson, P.O. Box 568, Abingdon, VA 24210.

Chesapeake Writers Conference. Rick Ughetti, Director, Department of Continuing Education, Rappahannock Community College, South Campus, Glenns, VA 23149.

Shenandoah Valley Writers' Guild. Geneva I. Nasworthy, Director, RFD 1, Box 217-A2, Woodstock, VA 22664.

Tidewater Writers' Conference. Agnes W. Thomas, Director, 1415 Meads Road C, Norfolk, VA 23505.

Highland Summer Conference. Dr. Grace Toney Edwards, Director, Box 5917, Radford Univ., Radford, VA 24142.

Shenandoah Valley Playwrights Retreat. Paul Hildebrand, Jr., Director, S.V.P.R., Pennyroyal Farm, Box 167F, Route 5, Staunton, VA 24401.

Pennsylvania

Philadelphia Writers' Conference. Sheila Martin, Registrar-W, 28 Home Road, Philadelphia, PA 19003.

Writers' Workshop. Jeanette Rapp, Director, Continuing Education, Pittsburgh Theological Seminary, 616 N. Highland Avenue, Pittsburgh, PA 15206.

University of Pittsburgh Writers Conference. Fourth Floor, William Pitt Union, Pittsburgh, PA 15260.

Kentucky

Appalachian Writers Workshop. Mike Millins, Director, Hindman Settlement School, Hindman, KY 41822.

Writing Workshop for People over 57. Roberta James, Director, Council on Aging, Ligon House, University of Kentucky, Lexington, KY 40506-0442.

Jesse Stuart Creative Writing Workshop. Kent Forrester, Director, Department of English, Murray State University, Murray, KY 42071.

Carter Caves Writer's Workshop. Lee Pennington, Director. Write Lois Glover, Department of Parks, Capital Plaza Tower, Frankfort, KY 40601.

Eastern Kentucky University Creative Writing Conference. William Sutton, Director, Department of English, Eastern Kentucky University, Richmond, KY 40475.

District of Columbia

Georgetown Writers Conference. Barbara Raskin and John Powers, Directors, SSCE, Suite 306 ICC, Georgetown University, Washington, D.C. 20057.

Washington Independent Writers Conference. Patricia DeYoung, Director, W.I.W., 525 National Press Building, Washington, D.C. 20045.

I Write in Order to Live

Betty Donley Harris

Betty Donley Harris

From the moment of my birth, tradition and society forced me to become a patient, loving, kind, feminine, possessed thing. I accepted that role and the fact that the male role was dominant. For years (it seems like thousands) I almost destroyed myself as a person trying to live up to that role, never taking any time for myself even though I continued to grow inwardly where no one could see. Everything I did centered around my home, husband, and sons. Sometimes to relieve my feelings I would write them down. I was a closet writer.

After a good—by many standards—marriage of forty-two years, my husband died suddenly after being retired only one year. My life changed completely. I was never prepared to be on my own and be responsible for myself. I thought I needed someone to take care of me. But I soon discovered resources I never knew I had, and through this experience I was evolving again into who I really am. I liked myself more than I ever had.

For one year I kept very busy but hurting internally because of the loss of my mate and battling my loneliness, needing male companionship and sensual fulfillment. One morning when the hurt became almost unbearable, with tears streaming, I started to write to my deceased husband. I wrote and wrote, pulling out all of the memories and what I was feeling. I discovered it was great therapy and I am still writing.

I attended a poetry workshop on the campus of West Virginia University in Morgantown where I live. When I found myself actually in the room where the workshop was held I wondered what on earth I was doing there. I vowed to sit in the corner and just listen. My experience in Maggie Anderson's poetry workshop was earthshaking to say the least and such a tremendous release.

I could write and it was not too bad! It was as is I were born again into another body and for the first time in my life I felt good about being me, a unique, interesting person with some talent of my own. I don't think there are any words to describe that "mountain-top" feeling which continued for about three months. I saw poetry everywhere. I wrote and wrote and wrote about everything. I would awaken early in the morning with phrases, ideas, and whole lines pushing me out of bed to grab a pencil and paper. I wrote on grocery lists, church bulletins, scraps of paper or anything available. All of the feelings held back for sixty-two years were pouring out and it was wonderful and exciting. I didn't feel inferior to others and could converse with people easily for the first time in my life.

I am still learning, growing, and evolving into my real self. I find I am happiest when I am in any kind of a learning experience, be it a classroom, lecture, or just reading or writing. Time passes swiftly and I started late. It is so great to continue to grow. I do not expect to be a great writer and do not write for a living but write in order to live!

I would like to write about the problem of sexuality and the older woman. I am still trying to deal with that and welcome any answers. This poem speaks of these feelings.

HIS PILLOW

Once you cradled the head of a prince
and I rested and rocked in the strength of him.
Red and ripe were his lips
Trembling twin apples
tempted me to taste
and I did
again and again
I consumed.

Now my appetite reaches out
to enfold you into my body
to quench my thirst
and you are empty
A bucket without cool water
once so full
spilling over
Damn! Why did he die?

Woman, past your prime
Why is there still a need?
I should be in my burial box
Why do I feel so young
trapped in this wrinkled vessel?
A seed not fertilized
withering of thirst
among new pregnant orchards
and green growing grass
Still holding soft young dreams
within my barren pod.

—Betty Donley Harris

●

Sitting There: The Discipline of Writing

Maggie Anderson

Maggie Anderson

Eric Goodman

Talking about the discipline of writing isn't much fun. Flannery O'Connor said, "I suppose half of writing is overcoming the revulsion you feel when you sit down to it." Usually, that "revulsion" is quickly eradicated as one begins to enjoy the process: the story that wants to be told, the play of words against each other, the search for the accurate and unusual image. But it's much more fun to talk about these kinds of things, or to talk about poems that seem to come through magical inspiration than to talk about the requisite hard work and devotion that must precede them. It's more interesting and exciting to talk about the happy accident of a resonant word than to talk about writing a page a day without fail. And yet the truth, as any writer knows, is that writing , as any other art, requires constant vigilance and a lot of practice. In writing of Sylvia Plath, Adrienne Rich tells us that Plath knew "that to be a writer means discipline, indefatigable commitment, and a passion for hard work"—no less than that.

In trying to discipline ourselves to do the hard work necessary to making art, most of us have I think two general tendencies that can interfere. One is to demand too much of ourselves given the actual circumstances of our everyday lives. This is particularly common for writers who are nearly constantly occupied with the physical, emotional, and intellectual demands of earning a living, or of bearing or rearing children (i.e., most women writers). But even just fifteen minutes a day will yield something after awhile. That we have too little time is no reason to assume that we have *no* time. Tillie Olsen, our most valuable writer on why writers don't write, reminds us again and again to keep alive as much as we can realistically given the actual circumstances of our lives. She acknowledges that this will sometimes be, necessarily, "partial, occasional . . . or . . . only intention, aspiration." When circumstances thwart or limit the work, it is extremely important to remember that that does not mean that we should abandon it entirely, that we were not "really meant to be a writer." Our task is to remain committed while seeing our human limitations clearly and making generous allowance for them. Olsen quotes William James: "The world can and has been changed by those to whom the ideal and the real are dynamically contiguous."

A second, seemingly contradictory, tendency that can interfere with our disciplining ourselves is that we, often, do not demand enough. Another way of putting this— probably the more accurate way— is that we do not give ourselves permission to take our art seriously enough to consider it "work" and, therefore, a thing we must report to daily. Knowing that we are working regularly and well—not because anyone required it but because we said it was important and worthwhile and wanted to do it—can yield an almost giddy sense of potency. It is the sense of personal power that comes from having exercised internal control, from having made up the rules ourselves and then followed them. It's the feeling many people have when they are successful in losing weight or in breaking a drug habit. But in order to exercise this kind of control one must first believe in the value of the end product as well as the intrinsic worth of the process (even if no product is immediately forthcoming). In order to discipline oneself to write regularly and seriously, one must first believe profoundly in the value of the writing. Tillie Olsen puts it this way: "How much it takes to become a writer. Bent (far more common than we assume), circumstances, time, development of craft—but beyond that: how much conviction as to the importance of what one has to say, one's right to say it. And the will, the measureless store of belief in oneself to be able to come to, cleave to, find the form for one's own life comprehensions." And she adds, "Difficult for any male not born into a class that breeds such confidence. Almost impossible for a girl, a woman."

It is easier in our society to obtain forgiveness than permission and we often apply this principle to ourselves as well. It is easier to forgive ourselves for lack of discipline than to give ourselves permission to exercise the kind of good discipline that accepts the value of our work and meets its demands for concentrated attention.

The following "rules for discipline" come from my own struggles with it—ongoing struggles. I want to share a few things that I have found helpful in trying to discipline myself to write in both favorable and unfavorable circumstances, in times when I believed in my worth as a writer and times when I didn't.

(1) *Discipline yourself realistically*. If you have, literally, only ten or fifteen minutes a day in which you can get off alone and write, set yourself only that demand. Fifteen minutes may seem inconsequential but it will eventually yield something—if only the realization that you need more time, and perhaps the courage to demand more of those around you who might help to make that possible. It's probably wise to begin any schedule of disciplined writing on a small scale anyway. It's better to give yourself room to grow into than to set yourself up for failure by making out a work schedule that you can't possibly stick to.

(2) *Everything matters*. Don't assume that in that fifteen minutes, or even an hour, you must be actually making up a poem or writing chapter twenty of your novel. If you are a writer, all the writing that you do matters. In your allotted time period (or if your allotted space— some writers work better around the "page a day" rule) write anything you want to write that is important to you. If you feel like writing a journal entry or a few unrelated sentences—impressions of the day, or the room, or the sky—do that. It's all writing and it all "counts."

Although "everything matters" and "everything counts" beware of using your precious time to write to clear off your desk. Writers often exercise a great deal of craft, persuasiveness and subtle wit, for example, in writing business letters, but this is not the kind of writing to do during your time to write. This can become a particular temptation at a certain stage in a writer's development when there are a lot of things that look like the real writing work but are not. Sending work out to be published, writing letters to find out what happened to the work you sent out to be published, or retyping work are writing-related

In order to discipline oneself to write regularly and seriously, one must first believe profoundly in the value of the writing.

activities that are valuable to one's writing life, but they are essentially secretarial tasks that can better be done at another time. They will not yield that sense of having done the real work that devoting a certain period of time each day to one's private writing will.

(3) *Indulge your eccentricities.* One of the biggest difficulties in sticking with any work schedule is that it can become predictable, stale. Sometimes breaking out of that stagnant feeling of having done this already yesterday and the day before can be accomplished by a simple variation in tools, or place, or position. Try, for example, writing with a different color pen, or with a different pen for different days or feelings. Get a new notebook. Write on the page upside down or sideways. Write in a different place—unlikely places are sometimes helpful, like under your desk, in a closet, in a coffee shop, in the basement, in your car. Sometimes, if you have a very comfortable work place, making yourself deliberately a little bit uncomfortable will jar some sedentary part of you loose and end in some interesting writing. Sometimes writing at a desk, in a straight chair, can have unpleasant associations with other kinds of work. Separating yourself from that association can help the writing. I found, for example, when was working a forty hour a week desk job (work totally unrelated to my writing) it helped me to stand up to write. Standing up made me "feel like a writer;" sitting down at my desk made me "feel like a civil servant."

(4) *Give yourself rewards that relate to the effort.* If one works in a factory, one wants a raise in pay for good work, not a gold star on a chart such as children get in school. Rewards are only meaningful if they are appropriate to the activity. If I'm rewarding myself for good disciplined writing, for sticking to my schedule, I've found that dinner out or a movie is not as satisfying as a reward that's more closely related to the writing itself. Buy yourself a new pen—or, better yet, for phenomenal achievement, a new typewriter. Give yourself a break from the writing one day and go to the library, or buy yourself a book you've coveted. Relating the reward to the specific activity is also another way of testifying to its seriousness. A lot of people can "earn" a night on the town; only serious writers "earn" new typewriters. It's important to be judicious with your rewards. They will probably lose their impact if they are too frequent or too easy to obtain. To do their job (which is to make you feel even more pleased with yourself and with the writing) they must feel like a real privilege, and they must relate to the work for which they are reinforcement.

(5) *Occasionally break your schedule entirely.* One of the best intrinsic rewards of any kind of self-imposed rule comes from knowing that you can, sometimes, break it. It's important that rules not be broken too early in establishing any kind of writing discipline, but probably after several weeks of hard work it's a good idea to give yourself a day off—maybe even if you don't think you "need it." I've found that it's better to give myself the day off consciously and in advance. Again, it's easier to forgive ourselves for breaking a rule than to give ourselves permission to break it, but, particularly when you are making all your own rules (when you are, simultaneously, legislator, law enforcement officer, and latent criminal), it's better to give permission. You'll enjoy

it more and you won't be dogged by several unproductive days of self-recrimination.

(6) *Avoid punitive metaphors.* Any metaphor (like "chaining yourself to the desk") sounds distasteful, or even punitive, seems bound to end in failure. One disciplines oneself in writing (or any other art form) in order to clarify, to give voice to the concerns of the heart and the mind. Doing that is a demanding activity and a self-revealing one. But, most of the time, it is a joyous one as well. A discipline that comes from an internal belief in the inherent value of the activity will be liberating, not confining, and the metaphors we use to describe that discipline should not be confining either. Perhaps the best metaphors are those that encompass a kind of anticipatory patience because much of disciplined writing does have to do with just sitting there, "being," as is said of fortunate job hunting, "in the right place at the right time."

Finally, discipline in writing is only important at all so that, as Flannery O'Connor says, we'll be "sitting there the day it would come well." Those days are their own incomparable reward.

●

Those days are their own incomparable reward.

The Necessities We Live

The Editors

Journal Entry: *I have dreams coming home late, alone. First, that the dog, long dead, will run from the bushes into the beam of my headlights with glad barks. And, coming home, late at night, alone, I dream the dream of the gift. From the mailbox, an envelope will give news of a legacy. Money, the bills silken and heavy like stationery. Or perhaps my son has scribbled a phone message. "New York publisher wants your book. Money on the way."*

The dream of making my life is a longer dream that I have drafted over and over again. Fix the roof, fifteen hundred dollars. A hundred a month toward kids' college. Storm windows, $19 each, for my bedroom. Sleep late, winter sun playing on my blanket. Take up the carpets in my house, put in wood floors. Silence the heater. Buy a car. Stay up late. I would fix the plumbing and go see my sister in Italy. I would have the chimney cleaned. I would talk or swim or run each day; serve at Manna Meal once a week; read books. I'd finish the quilt for my bed.

I would take my time and in taking my time make my life my own. I would finish chapter 5B of The Wicked Women and write 6 and 7, each of which I have rehearsed in my mind, but now I can't stand to think about them any more. They need to be written. And the Whirlwind Stories, already wound within me, need only to be rewound on paper.

I dream these things each time I enter my dirt road, especially at night, and alone. That, after the return of the dog, there will be an envelope, or perhaps a message left by my son, and I can begin writing the long dream of roofs and heaters, winter sun and cats whose owners have moved away, and a dog, the dream of wood floors as pretty as the young skin I'll never have again, sunlight, and the stories coming like shopping lists from the necessities I live.

—Faith Holsaert

Journal Entry: *Eating a decent lunch. A simple thing like this makes me feel sane again. Forget the higher pleasures. Just to have the grace to take the time to go off and eat a decent lunch by myself with this book is an accomplishment anymore. Cauliflower and rice and roast beef and a roll and coffee. Just to have the grace to remember whether I ate breakfast or not this morning (o.j.) is a treasure. Bliss would be time to meditate. I need someone to wash my dishes, clean my house, iron my clothes, put my storm windows up, make me a salad. Someone to buy me a blue suit and a new pair of stockings. Someone to rub my shoulders and back.*

What you must do to be a writer: write, keep spading up words; read ("Your favorite poet of the week"); cultivate a knowledge and appreciation of the other arts. What a blessing it would be if I could just do my dishes, sew up the hem of my skirt, the hole in my pocket.

Something big is brewing.

—from *Collecting Myself: A Journal*—Christine Beregi

Christine Beregi's journal entry, with its suggestion of transmutation, is brought to fulfillment in her poem "I Am." The definition of brew is to prepare by steeping, and so Beregi's final sentence with its homey and apt metaphor speaks for all woman artists who prepare for the pursuit of their art through immersion into daily life.

The tension between the sense of "Something big is brewing" and "The necessities we live," in the words of Faith Holsaert, Charleston writer, is a major concern of the woman artist. How does one produce art and children and nurture both? What are the lessons to be learned when women attempt to combine their lives and their art? Can they be separated? It seems these questions are central to our lives as both artists and women because in trying to answer them we may come to an understanding of what underlies our art, and how our impulses and visions—of our lives and our art—are shaped into realities.

Kate Harward, a potter from Belington, and mother of eight writes, "The work is always in balance with what is cooking on the stove or whether the diapers in the machine will dry in the rain today. Or perhaps a child desperately unhappy for some reason, or maybe a husband's understated plea for not another late night. Balancing the work this way is definitely not the stereotyped vision of an artist. It is the way I keep both sides of me healthy."

But this balance is often hard won as the responsibility for the dailiness of life can mute the creativity of the homemaker/artist. Bristol craftwoman Carol Shinn-Schweiker's poem, "Today, the Sheets" expresses clearly the deferment of art for the role of homemaker/mother.

Her generous perspective is echoed by almost all our artists, many of whom noted that when children are small and the demands greater, the mother/artist must always be on the lookout for ways to meld the artistic life with the everyday one. Harward, whose pottery studio workshop is attached to her home, reflects, "Looking closer at what that means to my work, I think I never separate myself from the home and the family."

Helen Bratt, a painter from Charleston, seconds this. "I can paint any place. I have painted in my kitchen, my dining room, indoors and outdoors." She suggests: "Keeping a painting on which I am working within sight of the sink and stove helps me study it while I am cooking or doing dishes. Then when I can clear the time to paint I have solved some of my problems and can proceed with my painting . . . There are many household tasks in which we use our hands but our minds are free to create."

The presence of children in one's artistic life, still not a usual thing for the male artist, leads to improvisations in work space and to changes in the direction of one's art. "When the kids were babies," recalls Carolyn Sanders-Turner of Beckley, "I switched medium from oils to watercolors as I was concerned about their safety. They were always welcome to paint too, but as I worked in the home they were there with me."

Jan Hoffman, a fiber artist living outside Cincinatti, writes: "Most of my work is done while sitting in an idling car (I'm a creative chauffeur), on line at the supermarket (a super place to market one's work), or at the dentist's trying to make my fabric lambs faster than he can replace bands on my children's teeth. I finish pillows at the PTA, fiber lions while doing laundry, and weave while waiting for my floors to dry."

I Am

verdure of pine spinning into darkness;
weave of roots and reeds and fibers,
phloem and xylem pulsing,
tumbling on a plateau of time.
I am wind chimes tinkling
on the porch of an abandoned house;
an uninhabited room spawning shadows at
  dusk;
woman standing at a dark window
above a neon-lit boulevard.
I am sunset pooling on the wall
behind a huddle of businessmen;
candlelight in a flourescent-lit room.
I am kindling wood,
knotted and laced with embering grains;
a chipped earthen vessel holding rain;
song of steeple bells
mauled above the blasts of trucks in traffic.
I am the face of a woman
seen through shields of glass
clouded with reflections.

—Christine Beregi

Pam Boggess

Judy Canty

Despite the years when all energies seem devoted to children and husband and other worlds, our artists feel this is not time and energy lost; rather they are growing and increasing their awareness for future creative expression. "Since the birth of my daughter in 1982 I have produced almost no "creative writing," Bonni V. McKeown, author of *Peaceful Patriot* and other works, writes. "But my observation eye has kept open the whole time, and the more life I live, the more I will have to say when I do start writing. I don't feel blocked or deadened; rather my creativity has gone into other channels and will resurface as writing."

This "resurfacing" of new relationships with our homes, our families, and ourselves is explored by poet Martha Miles of Morgantown. "I had always thought of myself as a person who would make her mark on the world through her mind, never through her hands. Every artistic project I attempted using my hands had a decidedly third-grade quality. I had trouble sewing: my stitches were uneven, hems hung lopsidedly, I stuck myself with pins. So I swore off painting, sculpture, and all crafts. It was therefore quite a surprise to find that, beginning with my first pregnancy, I had an urge to create things with my hands. found myself making crib animals for babies, wreaths for my doors, play dough, and smocked dresses for my daughter. And loved it. I made bread for the family and reveled in the kneading and its rising. The children and I made ornaments for Christmas, all of which still hang proudly from our trees. My lack of talent didn't matter. I made those things for a private forum, my family, and it was a forum not interested in artistic standards. There will probably never be a poem I write that will feel as proud of as I am of those ornaments or Christmas cookies. It's a show I wouldn't have missed for anything."

Finally, as all artist/mothers seemed to emphasize, one comes to see that these years are really few. "A mother considers the total picture and spends her life ordering the composition so that she can pass on some meaning to her children. Sometimes a great deal of poetic license is required for this task. A mother's glimpse of the future puts the elements of the present in perspective," writes Diana Wohl, a sculptor, now living in Stowe, Ohio. "As my children become older, and more independent, the time for actual production for my art will reemerge, yet I'm convinced that their contribution to my creativity in the long run will more than justify the hours of nurturing that fill my days for now."

This art that creates the atmosphere which refreshes the spirit is celebrated by Gail Adams, Morgantown writer. "She showed me how to hold a plate with its fragile weave up to the light and see my hand outlined on glaze. Taught me to test goblets to see if they were capable of song. She sat flowers on the table and their color lit the linens up. This was a picture she'd painted, a setting for a still life of polished apples, lozenged ham, potatoes rilled with green. Leaning down to light the candles, pouring cocoa in the morning, wiping tears and noses in the afternoon, my mother, who would be amazed to be called artist, transformed our lives with her art."

This nurturing and the joy with which the artist passes on her art to her family is cherished. The aesthetic impulse can become a structure: "We designed and built our own home," writes sculptor Susan Wood of Leon. "It grew from our creative drive and need for expression. It is rooted in our way of life. Our home is a monolithic structure of natural stone, wood and stained glass. The stone came from our land. We searched old buildings for wood and slate floorings, for beams, for marble basins, for wrought iron and glass. It is a tactile house. Its spaces flow and change as life moves in and out of them. It breathes. It has clarity." And the home reflects the respect for the artist who lives there. "My family has always been a source of inspiration to me," Wood writes. "They took me seriously." And when an artist is taken seriously, the life and the art combine and the life itself becomes a creation.

Today, the Sheets

*I wanted to paint today, instead I changed
the sheets.*

*Twenty years ago I began to write a ballet
theme,
instead I fell in love and so began the
rhythm of sheet changing*

*Awakening this morning to strains of The
New World Symphony, knowing
that each soul writes
his own song regardless of the
sheets changed, I
can only cry out to my
children to bear witness
that creativity is the challenge
of opening eyes
and singing songs and painting as you dance to make
the bed.*

*Despite the less than more, I would not
change it.*

—Carol Ann Shinn Schweiker

Creative Ambiguity

Ruth Frazier

Ambiguity. Layers of meaning—richness and complexity and an understanding of these, the ability to encompass uncertainty and doubt. Ambiguity is the condition for all creative activity. Without the tension of ambiguity, no creative efforts would be made. Ambiguity generates energy.

Women know about ambiguity: the wave swell of ocean—ebb and flow—the movement resulting from tidal turbulence. We know the seething billows of pain on which our children are born. For us, nothing is simple, nothing without the awareness of the numberless distractions leading to creativity and growth. Ambiguity is a source of energy and expansion. Loving a child who does something of which we disapprove or which we cannot initially understand leads us to broader tolerance rather than to denial of that child. Resentment flowers along with love. Out of the tension of ambiguous situations we grow.

We know these things, yet sometimes deny them. Women are puzzled and put down by authority, knitting their brows over bold statements claiming truth and certainty, remaining silent. We often fail to raise the legitimate question, feeling tentative in the face of authority. We perceive ambiguity as a failing rather than a source of strength. Accused of being ambiguous or ambivalent, we wonder if we really don't know our own minds.

We must be wary of the ways in which such terms are used. We must reclaim and redefine them in more positive, illuminating ways. Ellen Goodman is wary when she writes in a 1979 column: "I've always been uneasy with people who think ambiguity a weakness and ambivalence a flaw."

We women know about complexity. There are no easy answers where our lives are concerned. Yet life's complexities do not keep us from making decisions. We make them all the time, hut we acknowledge that such decisions are neither final nor irrevocable, that different situations require different responses. Even if we have not raised children, we are accustomed to the changing rhythms and needs of our bodies and how predictable/unpredictable things can be. We are affected by changes in the weather, and wonder how some people seem unmoved, unchanged by the ceaselessly moving and sensuous external world. We feel a great deal of conflict in our lives, and, as Goodman asserts, we need to speak of these.

Yet we bear within us the knowledge that our rhythms are meaningful and creative.

> It's important to raise the conflicts many of us feel, even if that means breaking rank with someone else's definition of consistency. If this leaves us open to the charge of inconsistency, or vulnerable to the simplistic attack of those who believe in force rather than choice, so it goes. It's not important to pass some moral purity test set up by others.

It *is* important to share, reflect on, and continually reassess our own complex, internal standards. Yet we allow ourselves to be silenced, to feel weak because we don't categorically assert *the truth* about a complex issue. We feel the put-down of force and power against our flesh, and we remain silent. Among ourselves we do the important business of sharing, reflecting, reassessing our internal standards, and in this essential dialogue we grow in understanding and strength.

We feel ambiguous; we don't know *the* answers. Good! We feel all the separate possibilities that inform reality; we are vulnerable to all aspects of things; we cut nothing off, exclude no potential. Good! We suspect it takes blindness and a limited sensibility to assert absolutes, and in our hearts we suspect and impugn certainties. Good! To hold ambiguity close rather than accept easy solutions, to cherish our doubts and celebrate the richness in things: these are the "truths" of our everyday lives.

When we focus on ambiguity in a positive light, we know it as essential to creativity—whether of ideas, works of art, or the resolution to personal problems. We realize that there are as many perceptions of things as there are perceivers. And we confess that we often compromise in the world, serving grace instead of honesty when we work in places and along lines that deny our true perceptions and rhythms. Yet we bear within us the knowledge that our rhythms are meaningful and creative.

We find ourselves in situations where people don't listen to each other, where communication fails. We feel pain in that process and try to redeem things by moving out along all the separate lines of thought, trying to draw them together somehow. We readily accept ambiguity; what we can't bear is the lack of sensitivity that keeps people from hearing other opinions. We move away from such encounters, knitting our brows, carrying the dialogue forward alone, still seeking to negotiate the issues inside ourselves. We wish we had answers, for we feel the need to rest in certaintly at times, but we know the meaning we rest in today is temporary and that tomorrow we will move through further tensions towards more expanded meanings.

The Alternative to Ambiguity

What is the alternative to assuming ambiguity as the natural rhythm for creativity? Opting for certainty while knowing it to be partial truth masking itself as the whole truth? Such "knowing" gives a false sense of security. We know there is no ultimate security in life, that life's meaning is contained within the parameters of death, and that this knowledge in itself creates ambivalence and ambiguity. Miriam Shapiro, in an essay from *Working It Out* admits to feeling anxious each time she enters her studio. Alone and fearful, she faces the blank canvas. She confronts death and her responsibility and need to create life in the face of it.

We women know experientially that we are mortal and that we must overcome even the finality of death by continuing to press our life urges upon matter and substance. We survive; we more than survive—we create. We realize our strengths. Shapiro says: "An individual overcomes the fear of death by working. As long as I work I maintain life . . . after death, work will 'stand in' for by being."

For us, nothing is simple, nothing without the awareness of the numberless distractions leading to creativity and growth.
Ambiguity is a source of energy and expansion.

Simone de Beauvoir, in *The Ethics of Ambiguity*, speaks about the ways in which women are thought to be childlike and treated accordingly. Across many cultures, women submit to the truths, laws, gods, and customs of men. They take shelter in the shadow of men, adopting men's opinions and values without argument. Says de Beauvoir,

> Once there appears a possibility of liberation (for women),
> it is resignation of freedom not to exploit the possibility
> a resignation which implies dishonesty and which is a
> positive fault.

For her, existence is fraught with ambiguity, and to attain truth, one must not dispel the ambiguity, but "accept the task of realizing it."

We are dishonest when we fail to take on and realize our freedom. Shouted down or intimidated by authority, criticized for being wishy-washy, we become silent. This silence and resignation preclude a vital dialectic between the sexes. The cost is great and we know it, both to ourselves and our work, yet we pay it often. We become mute, abrogating our vision when our ways of seeing and knowing things are not recognized as satisfying the going standards of certainty in our culture. We women are wary of facticity. Good! Facts hold in stasis those who prize them. Yet our silence implies acceptance. Or we speak a language not our own. In contrast to the voice of authority, ours sounds weak, uncertain, filled with qualification and question. So we change our tune; we adopt men's modes and manners and assume the voice of assertiveness, and that is a mistake. Women who achieve success by adopting men's values and attitudes know in their hearts the cost of such success.

The Necessity of Failure

Becoming silent and assuming the voice of another—both deny the ambiguity at the heart of all interpretations of both success and failure. What's needed is a reassessment of what constitutes success for each of us in our many activities, the articulation of the diverse and complex ways in which success and failure differ for us all. We women know that failure is necessary, it is endemic to life. Sometimes our dinners are successful, sometimes the same ingredients fail us; we taste our food as we cook it and admit our failures, learning how to overcome them the next time around. Yet out in the world, away from our kitchens, we tend to denigrate the taste and savor of failure. We fear disapprobation. Yet we know that failure often illuminates problems and leads to the new. The artist knows that if she does not keep her eye on the emerging process, ready to see and respond to lapses in vision or technique, the finished product will lack integrity. Meanings are not given in advance; the meaning of a work of art emerges from the interaction between the artist and the medium; it is a meaning continuously disclosed. In retrospect, we often thank our failures for keeping us honest and alive.

About success and failure there is much ambiguity. What succeeds for one doesn't do for another; what fails for one is promise for another. Good! Would we want it otherwise? As a teacher, I delight in the sheer pleasure of holding up a work of literature to the vision of many minds, turning it around and around until we've extracted as much of the

Rosemary Serian

"Composition in B&W"

essential oil as we can, knowing there is always more richness and complexity. As Aristotle saw so clearly with respect to ancient tragedy, a complex plot is more beautiful and interesting than a simple one. Our inability to fix a final meaning to things does not diminish our joy in life or work; rather, it enhances things. We delight in changing seasons. We don't like to exist in a static, constant state. We thrive on contrast and diversity. The beauty of a gemstone is expressed by turning it again and again, allowing it to reflect its radiance in all directions. We love prisms!

For me, there has always been a great deal more frustration attached to such things as multiple choice tests where one answer, and one only, is possible than to expressive, essay tests. In multiple choice questions all the answers seem likely depending upon how you interpret the question, and my delight stems from trying to "fit them all in." It's the same with analogy tests; it's more fun making the analogies between disparate things than trying to figure what specific answer the testmakers had in mind. Figuring new analogies is what makes poetic metaphor.

We women don't always do very well when things are supposed to be simple; we are told we complicate matters when we see multiple meanings and create from that tension. We find ourselves pressured into making hasty decisions, and we make them, often very well, only to be accused of lacking a logical sensibility. We are intuitive. Good! We love life more than the "ruthless concentration to work which leads to satisfactory achievement," as Amelie Rorty described it in *Working It Out*. Good! We are not ruthless. Rorty suggests that when "the perfection of the work threatens the perfecting of our lives, we almost automatically, though often unwillingly, gravitate to what will sustain life." Good! Why not choose life over work, and are they really separate things? Does one have any real meaning apart from the other? Women, notoriously unable to separate life from work from love, perhaps should be redefining just exactly what "satisfactory achievement" means. We make decisions all the time, and it is in the dialectic of conflicting priorities and claims that we come to experience growth. Because of the many levels on which we live our lives, we women find it hard to think in terms of that resignation of freedom of which deBeauvoir speaks. Such resignation would sit under authority unmurmuring, unmoving. We are seldom given to sit long anywhere!

The Rhythms of Ambiguity

Out of the tension of ambiguity we continue to rise to the stimulus of work. We move to ease and resolution. And with each new solution we are aware of a new beginning, not merely an end; what now feels right becomes the nexus for new tensions and new problems to be solved. We survive and expand the meaning of our life and work. We become strong.

Nietzsche loved his enemies for they made him strong. Because they held other opinions, saw the world differently, he grew more in his encounters with them than with those who placidly agreed with him. People towards whom we feel indifference bring us no creative friction; they make us feel nothing. Nietzsche also said, "You must have chaos in your soul to give birth to a dancing star." By that he did not mean confusion without issue, but rather a hard, honest affirmation of all the real and irreducible ambiguities that exist and that spark activity. From finality, facticity, certainty; from authority and dogma come nothing new. This is the place of death.

True uneasiness is living along the straight line, where the goal determines the process, where *a priori* truths are accepted. Just as multiple choice tests make me uncomfortable, so does all this talk about goal-setting. The assumption is that if you posit the end, you then move to secure the means to realize that end. As though we raised children in the constant light of a pre-determined image of adulthood. As if we did not know that ends are constantly altered during the process of pursuing them! So long as they are loosely, tentatively defined, goals stimulate beginnings, movements. If they are set in concrete, creativity becomes the handmaiden rather than the inventor. The end or goal of anything is disclosed during the act of creating; we women know these things.

We play many roles, wear many masks, but they all belong to us and we are reflected through all of them. Our rhythms permit us to move from solitude to love; we nourish ourselves alone and with friends and lovers; we move from doubt to temporary certainty and back again to doubt. Good! We move with far greater ease when we accept the rhythms of ambiguity.

We know about ambiguity, the wash of fear and thrill of pleasure, the anger towards other succeeded by the rush of love through the heart, the warming and chilling, the layers of meaning that run through our lives and elude final explanation. Though we can't always give the answers, life is not meaningless or absurd. de Beauvoir makes this final distinction for all of us:

> To declare that existence is absurd is to deny that it can ever be given meaning; to say that it is ambiguous is to assert that its meaning is never fixed, that it must be constantly *won*.

Let us try to assume our fundamental ambiguity.

So long as they are loosely, tentatively defined, goals stimulate beginnings. If they are set in concrete, creativity becomes the handmaiden rather than the inventor.

Finding the Marmalade

While we weren't looking
Mother made this
all night in the Wearever
peaches swam &
beaded peel
her darkening brocade
Dad said "look at the orange Mama   "
& before bed she'd go down to stir

where is the long enamelled spoon
the pale page printed with citrus smear
sink, ice box, stove
her thumb went everywhere
& I went around with a rag
erasing

she didn't pride herself
fluting crusts in a shimmy of flour
once I gave her Millay for Christmas not potholders
she said now you're beginning to understand
stuttering children learned to read at her hand
navigate Amazons, stack the Sphinx
color Demeter cadmium red
but in the deeps of August
the Sound like lacquer
I'd be sandy just going through &
she'd be sitting there cutting up
coils of rind fall from yellow shears
wedding ring glossy with pulp
a messy business
& she artless
making it messier

out in the dark yard our dripping suits
hang on the line
the pungent citron rises through the house
wraps our juicy sleep

This isn't the recipe exactly
never anything the same way my mother
it isn't the family keeps it secret
    though it's always bitter when someone markets
    what you give freely & in private
but they forget or lose or don't care at the time
then later long for
    that suet pudding at the Huey Place
    sort of white wasn't it? no, not a carrot pudding
    plump raisins, no dusted figs, no plums enormous plums yes
    till the pudding becomes totally fictive, fat, Dickensian
    winking up from the darkling past, Aunt Anna's cellar
    carried forever over the river and through our snow
    past the hitching post
    into the holiday house

after my mother grew out of our kitchen
    though Dad dreamed her there once &
    was flooded with unbearable happiness
I lost the recipe
never having made it myself
she took it with her ha ha said her friends not meaning harm
& I find her there too
alive alive-O
fine tuned to each season
how in the deeps of July
a sudden yellow leaf curves down
you catch a breath from fall fields far ahead
while summer boils to its quintessence
on Right Front
your low flame
blue & steady

O Gratuitous concoction
older than the Chaldees!
the Magi thought they thought it up
to ring my crib with dense jars shining
sunlight the jewel
to honor the moment
the mystery of paraffin my first idea of preservation
I'd pry the wax up, eat it straight
& later, for an empty apartment
she'd give me a jar
wrapped in foil, say keep this upright
    she'd dispensed with paraffin, added nuts, left the tops open
I'd be daughter annoyed, one more thing
among so many givens
the slap dash & essential present

113

We never eat up these secret ingredients
patterns. prints
our suits on the line in the warm dark
salt water in the middle ear
  catch in the throat from going under
her flat steps around the magic triangle
sink, ice box, stove
three legged oracle matching her gait
to the bubble of fruit
the grit of the sweet
the vital syrup

Dad says he dreams the smell
amber with our lost summers
all night the cauldron turns its gold
the peel grows light under the lid
& woolly peaches glaze like pitch
stitching the hot quilt
translucent

It is the summer the war ends
in the photo I dig sand with this spoon
for the cup she scoops lumped sugar from its drum with
"There goes the ferry to Fort Slocum"
at her feet, I don't look, that is,
I don't know where to look
my father is taking this picture
she has left her thumbprint on
stuck in the Pocket Cook Book
on this page

  on this page old halos of honey apples, quince
  the ancient formula whereby
  over steady flame
  we claim
  the sour
  goes sweet
  though I'll never dig up all of this receipt
  because and even as I learn to love
  its clues.

—Devon McNamara

Peach Marmalade
(One Batch, More or Less)

3 oranges
6 peaches
9 cups water
9 cups sugar
1 cup coarsely chopped walnut meats

Wash fruit; cut in eighths; remove seeds and pulp from oranges; cut peel in thin strips; add pulp, water, and sugar; let stand overnight, stirring once or twice; boil slowly, stirring upon occasion, about two hours or until peel is tender and almost transparent. Add walnut meats. Pour into hot, sterilized jars, filling to top and fasten covers at once.

—Helen Steegar McNamara

Resources

Much of the information in this section was made available by the West Virginia Department of Culture and History, which is itself a most valuable resource to this state and region. More current information can be obtained from them at The Cultural Center, Capitol Complex, Charleston, West Virginia 25305. The resources here have been selected and arranged by Virginia Stelzig, Director of the Morgantown Public Library, with the help of Andrea Soccorsi, graduate student in English at West Virginia University. The bibliography is provided by Carol Bryan of Carol Bryan Imagines, Charleston.

Arts Institutions

Institutions maintain and administer an arts facility, have paid staff and a volunteer board of directors, and plan and present a year-round season of arts programs.

Actors Guild of Parkersburg
Abby Hayhurst, President
P.O. Box 881
Parkersburg, WV 26101
428-5961 (H) 485-0761 (O)

Aracoma Story
P.O. Box 2016
Logan, WV 25601
Liz Spurlock, President
752-7840

Berkeley County Civic Theatre
Stewart M. Borger, President
132 S. Queen Street
Martinsburg, WV 25401
263-3388 or 876-2291

Bluefield Area Arts and Crafts Center
500 Bland Street
Bluefield, WV 24701
Gene Basham, Director
325-8000
Marilyn Tinder, President
325-6650 (H)

Carnegie Hall, Inc.
Charles Goddard, Managing Director
105 Church Street
Lewisburg, WV 24901
645-7917

Clarksburg Art Center
P.O. Box 148
Clarksburg, WV 26301
Alice Mauk, President
622-9051 (Center)

Delf Norona Museum and Cultural Centre
801 Jefferson Avenue, P.O. Box 527
Moundsville, WV 26041
Richard Warmuth, President
845-8577
Susan Yoho, Director
843-1410 (O) 845-7145 (H)

Greenbrier Valley Theatre
Barbara Shaper, President
Box 494
Lewisburg, WV 24901
645-7847 (H) 645-3838 (Theatre)

Huntington Galleries
Roberta Emerson, Director
Park Hills
Huntington, WV 25701
529-2701

McCoy-McMechen Museum, Inc.
Tom Hawse, III, President
South Fork Road
Moorefield, WV 26836
538-6105 (O) 538-6396 (H)

Monongalia Arts Center
P.O. Box 239
Morgantown, WV 26505
Kerr Crosby, President
Beth Fiset, Executive Director
292-3325

Museum in the Community
Bobbie Hill, Director
Punam Arts Council
P.O. Box 251
Scott Depot, WV 25560
562-3645 (H)

Old Opera House Theatre
Liberty and George Streets
Charles Town, WV 25414
Hubert Rolling, Manager
725-4420 (Theatre)

Oglebay Institute
Stanley Coulling, Executive Director
Wheeling Park
Wheeling, WV 26003
242-4200 or 242-4744

Parkersburg Art Center
220 Eighth Street
Parkersburg, WV 26101
Jane Osborn, Director
Mark Fleming, Exhibits Coordinator
485-3859 or 485-3850 (O)

Sunrise Museums
J. Hornor Davis, IV, Executive Director
746 Myrtle Road
Charleston, WV 25314
344-8035 (O)

Youth Museum of Southern West Virginia
P.O. Box 1815
Beckley, WV 25801
Dave Beeman, President
255-6181 (O)
Karen Vuranch, Program Coordinator
252-3730 (Museum)

Arts Organizations

Arts organizations have non-profit status, a volunteer board of directors and sometimes a paid staff, and present local arts productions and sometimes national touring arts programs.

Dance

Appalachian Youth Jazz Ballet
Nina Denton, Artistic Director
P.O. Box 575
Charleston, WV 25322
343-6015 or 344-3654

Bluefield Dance Theatre
John R. Lamb
1801 Jefferson Street
P.O. Box 648
Bluefield, WV 24701
327-7616 (O)

Charleston Ballet
Andre Van Damme, Director
213 Hoyer Building, 901 Quarrier Street
Charleston, WV 25301
342-6541 (O)

Huntington Dance Workshop
c/o Mary Kessick
1430 7th Avenue
Huntington, WV 25701
522-7350 (O) 522-6446 (H)

Jerry Rose Dance Company
107 McTaggart Drive
Beckley, WV 25801
253-3497 (H) 255-5684 (O)

Morgantown Ballet
429 Beechurst Avenue
Morgantown, WV 26505
Bill Tomlinson, President
291-5299 (O)
Fiona Morris, Artistic Director
291-6141 (O)

Mountain Jazz Theatre
E. Moore Hall, Room 115
Morgantown, WV 26506
293-2080

New Steps and Movements, Inc.
Michael Harris
426½ Shrewburg Street, Suite 206
Charleston, WV 25301
343-6210

Rick Lee/WV Department of Culture and History

Beckley Dance Theatre

Orchesis
Mary Katherine Wiedebusch
E. Moore Hall, WVU
Morgantown, WV 26506
293-2080 (O) 296-3919 (H)

Parkersburg Civic Ballet
Norma Gunter
P.O. Box 4204
Parkersburg, WV 26104
428-2010

Vicki Dils Dance Theatre
P.O. Box 1712
Parkersburg, WV 26101
295-4302

Music

Buckhannon Chamber Orchestra
Patty Nay
Rt. 2, Box 204
Buckhannon, WV 26201
472-7983 (H)

Charleston Area Community Choir
Bruce E. Hogan, President
P.O. Box 20253
Charleston, WV 25302
925-6725 (H) or 345-6475

Charleston Civic Chorus
J. Truman Dalton
P.O. Box 2014
Charleston, WV 25327
766-3195 (O) or 766-1852 (H)

Charleston Symphony Orchestra
Shirley Furry, Manager
1210 Virginia Street, East
P.O. Box 2292
Charleston, WV 25301
346-6275 (H) or 342-0151 (O)

Charleston Symphony Youth Orchestra
Ellen Beal, President
130 Woodlands Drive
Nitro, WV 25143
755-7644 (H)

Charleston Conservatory of Music and Fine Arts
Suzanne Riggio, Administrator
University of Charleston
2300 MacCorkle Avenue
Charleston, WV 25304
344-4349

Choral Society of St. Albans
Peggy Jo Pridemore, Conductor
2258 Main Street
St. Albans, WV 25177
722-4198 (H)
Hunter O'Hara
727-2226 or 345-3176

Huntington Chamber Orchestra
Leland Thornburg, President
Huntington Galleries
Park Hills
Huntington, WV 25701
525-0404 (O)

Jubilee Chorale
Paul Blosser, Director
Homeland Avenue
Jane Lew, WV 26278
884-8112 (H)

Larry Parsons Chorale
Larry Parsons
Box 1076
Buckhannon, WV 26201
472-4292 (H) or 473-8000, Ext. 8466

Lilliput Orchestra
Suzanne Riggio, Manager
16 Terrace Road
Charleston, WV 25314
346-6095 (H) 344-4349 (O)

Harrison County Symphonic Chorus
Don Gardner
908½ S. Chestnut Street
Clarksburg, WV 26101
623-3397

Millbrook Chamber Orchestra
Henry Morrow, Jr.
Executive Director
Box 580, Entler Hotel
Shepherdstown, WV 25443
725-3441 or 876-3170

Parkersburg Choral Society
Mary Margaret Nuzum
110 Keyser Street
Marietta, OH 45750
(614) 373-7328

West Virginia Symphonette
Creative Arts Center, WVU
Morgantown, WV 26506
293-2901 (O)

Wheeling Symphony Orchestra
Susan Cox Nelson, Manager
Hawley Building, Suite 307
Wheeling, WV 26003
232-6191 (O)

Theatre

Appalachian Community Theatre
c/o Jim McCallum
P.O. Box 615
Madison, WV 25130
369-0511 (O) 369-1390 (H)

Apple Alley Players
Kris Peterson, President
Box 144
Keyser, WV 26726
788-3710 (H) 788-0788 (O)

Brooke Hills Playhouse
Sharon M. Harper, Coordinator
Box 186
Wellsburg, WV 26070
527-4359 (H) or 737-2922 (O)

Buckhannon Community Theatre
James Knorr
16 Gum Street
Buckhannon, WV 26201
472-5189 (H) or 472-3720 (O)

Charleston Light Opera Guild
James A. Thomas, President
P.O. Box 1762
Charleston, WV 26101
344-1641 (O) or 744-0264 (H)

Children's Theatre Bureau of Mid-Ohio Valley
Mary Ellen Kirkpatrick
5303 10th Avenue
Vienna, WV 26105
295-7129 (H)

Children's Theatre of Charleston
1105 Quarrier Street
Charleston, WV 25301
346-0164

Community Players, Inc.
Abbot Theatre
Judy Anderson
Box 1157
Huntington, WV 25701
525-0170 (Theatre)

Covered Bridge Playhouse
Ann Serafin
100 Keyes Avenue
Philippi, WV 26416
457-2415 (H) or 636-4120 (O)

Curtain Callers
Steve Bush, President
P.O. Box 1915
Beckley, WV 25802
253-1073 (H) or 877-3457

Eco Theatre
Maryat Lee
Rt. 1, Box 189
Hinton, WV 25951
466-5692 (O) or 466-2468

Hillbilly Players
Eileen Good
Newville, WV 26632
765-5469

Huntington Theatrical Ensemble
c/o Elaine Blue
1010 13th Street
Huntington, WV 25701
523-2147

Jubilee Theatre
Gerald Wood
Maxwell Run
Weston, WV 26452
269-5588 (H) or 269-5000 (O)

Kanawha Players
Box 4575
Charleston, WV 25304
Kathie Frank
Acting Managing Director
925-5051
Tom Craig, President
357-1766

Kith-N-Hills
Betty Lou Myers, President
103 Fairview
Ripley, WV 25271
372-6632

Mason County Community Theatre
Paula Barkey
103 English Road
Pt. Pleasant, WV 25550
675-4122 (H)

Music Hall Players
Paula Anderson, Business Manager
1015 Main Street
Wheeling, WV 26003
232-1170 (O) or (614) 676-1765

New Images
Bill Hairston
5316 Venable Avenue, SE
Charleston, WV 25304
925-9043 (H) or 342-3621 (O)

Parlor City Players
P.O. Box 36
New Martinsville, WV 26155

Petersburg Little Theatre
Vana Nespor
115 Virginia Avenue
Petersburg, WV 26847
749-7696 (H) or 257-4634 (O)

Pleasants County Players
c/o Ann Bradford
1017 Stadium Drive
St. Marys, WV 26170
784-3243 (H)

Puppet Mobile
West Virginia University
JoAnn Siegrist, Director
Creative Arts Center
Morgantown, WV 26506
293-2020

Putnam Theatre Company
Jerry Adkins
2636 Montana Avenue
Hurricane, WV 25526
562-9221 (H) or 344-8591 (O)

Sangod Theatre of Taylor County
John E. Stallings, Jr.
Vice President
305 Virginia Street
Grafton, WV 26354
265-3500 (O) 265-5398 (H)

Shakespeare Studio
Ann McNeil
907 Bridge Road
Charleston, WV 25314
347-5295 (O) 345-3752 (H)

Southern West Virginia Community College Theatre
Mrs. Joan Henry, Chairperson
Division of Humanities
Logan, WV 25601
752-5900

The Stage Door
c/o Phil Schenk
P.O. Box 24
Terra Alta, WV 26764

Summit Players
311 North Street
Bluefield, WV 24701
Peery Blackwell, President
327-8380 (O)

Theatre Associates of Huntington Galleries
c/o Jim Lawhorn
Park Hills
Huntington, WV 25701
529-2701 (O)

Theatre West Virginia
J.R. Wears, General Manager
Box 1205
Beckley, WV 25801
253-8313

Town and Country Players
Susanna Renahan, President
P.O. Box 1277
Morgantown, WV 26505
293-4808 (O) 296-3701 (H)

Town and Gown Players
Jo Ann Lough
Fairmont State College
Fairmont, WV 26554
367-4000 (O)

Town Theatre
Linda Simmons
Box 98
Hillsboro, WV 24946
653-4401 (H)

Towngate Theatre
Dee Dickison
Performing Arts Department
Oglebay Institute
Wheeling, WV 26003
242-4200 (O)

West Virginia Stageworks
Rebecca Kimmons
P.O. Box 2202
Charleston, WV 25328
348-2286 (O) 345-4217

Community Arts Councils

Community arts councils are primarily administered by volunteers who raise funds and present a season of arts programs for their communities.

Barbour County Arts and Humanities Council
Ann Serafin, President
100 Keyes Avenue
Philippi, WV 26416
457-2415 (H) or 636-4120 (O)

Berkeley County Council for the Arts
Richard Whiting
P.O. Box 782
Martinsburg, WV 25401
263-5046 (H)

Bethesda Community Artist Series
W. Brent Sturm
118 Bethesda Drive
Ona, WV 25545
743-3017 (H) or 736-0804 (O)

Bluefield Fine Arts Commission
Terry Wittington, President
1418 Montclair Street
Bluefield, WV 24701
327-8040 (H)

Boone County Arts Council
Sara Blizzard, President
40 Hickory Lane
Madison, WV 25130
369-2251

Braxton County Arts and Humanities Council
James Walker, President
601 Main Street
Sutton, WV 26601
765-7566

Brooke County Arts Council
Sharon Harper, President
P.O. Box 186
Wellsburg, WV 26070
527-4359 or 732-2992 (O)

Calhoun County Friends of the Arts
Tom McColley
Rt. 3, Box 325
Chloe, WV 25235
655-7429 (H)

Civic League of New Martinsville
Linda Oliver
170 Paddock Drive
New Martinsville, WV 26155
455-5828

Clarksburg/Harrison Cultural Foundation
John F. Skinner, President
226 Court Street
Clarksburg, WV 26301
622-5712

Clay County Arts Council
Sandra King
P.O. Box 356
Clay, WV 25043
587-2110 (H)

Fayette Fine Arts Festival
Carolyn Hill-Walther
231 Highland Avenue
Oak Hill, WV 25901
469-3551 (O) or 469-9366

Fairmont Arts and Humanities Council
Judy Byers, President
804 Coleman Avenue
Fairmont, WV 26554
366-5387 (H)

Fund for the Arts
Harold Graves, Director
818 Virginia Street, East
Charleston, WV 25301
345-0775 (O)

Grant County Arts Council
Vana Nespor, President
P.O. Box 988
Petersburg, WV 26847
749-7696 (H) or 257-4634 (O)

Greenbrier Valley Arts and Humanities Council
Mason Preston
224 West Court Street
Lewisburg, WV 24901
645-1223

Highland Arts Unlimited, Inc.
Dorothy Stephen, President
215 D Street
Keyser, WV 26726
788-1235 (H)

Jackson Arts Council
Ellen Pyles, President
P.O. Box 422
Ripley, WV 25271
372-4744 (H) or 372-6263 (O)

Jefferson County Arts Council
Melinda Sloate, President
P.O. Box 693
Shepherdstown, WV 25543
876-3515

Lincoln County Arts Council
Glenda Probst, President
325 Main Street
Hamlin, WV 25523
824-5705

McDowell Fine Arts Association
Kermit Grogen, President
Kimball, WV 24853
585-7564 (H)

Morgan Arts Council
Don Klein, President
Posey Hollow Road
Berkeley Springs, WV 25411
258-4009

Ohio Valley Arts Council
Paul Booz, President
61-14th Street
Wheeling, WV 26003
232-6810

Parkersburg Fine Arts Council
Damienne Dibble, Director
P.O. Box 1706
Parkersburg, WV 26102
428-3988

Pendleton County Committee for the Arts
Michelle Shomo, Vice President
Box 67
Franklin, WV 26807
358-2989 (H)

Pocahontas County Arts Council
Susan Burt
Marlinton Middle School
900 5th Avenue
Marlinton, WV 24954
799-6773 (O) or 799-6029 (H)

Putnam County Arts Council
Mary Barr Rhodes, President
103 Country Cove Estates
Scott Depot, WV 25560
757-7055 (H)

Randolph County Creative Arts Council
Donald Loher, President
Box 1819
Elkins, WV 26241
636-1900 (O) or 636-2372 (H)

Ritchie County Arts Council
Diane Scott
c/o Ritchie County Board of Education
217 W. Main Street
Harrisville, WV 26362
375-4715 (H) or 643-2220 (O)

River Cities Cultural Council
Matthew Neiburger, Executive Director
P.O. Box 1809
Ashland, KY 41105
(606) 329-1011 (O) or (606) 293-0124

Roane County Arts and Humanities Council
Charles Poole
107 Claude Street
Spencer, WV 25276
577-6731 (O) or 927-5228 (H)

Three Rivers Arts Council
Jim Gaitor
Talcott Post Office
Talcott, WV 24981
466-4100 (O)

Tri-City Fine Arts Association
Stephen Essof
716 Main Street
Sistersville, WV 26175
652-5661 (H) or 758-2331 (O)

Tug Valley Arts Council
Lois Bronson, Executive Director
P.O. Box 697
Williamson, WV 25661
235-1413 (H)

Upshur Arts Alliance
Jane Williams, President
1 Lincoln Heights
Buckhannon, WV 26201
472-3428

Weirton Area Arts Council
Robert Kaminski
4028 Pallisades Drive
Weirton, WV 26062
748-3356

Wyoming County Council for the Arts
Kathy Muscari, President
Box 357
Pineville, WV 24874
732-6870 (H)

Artists' Organizations

Individual artists' organizations represent groups of artists and present workshops, conferences, exhibitions, etc.

Allied Artists of West Virginia
Nancy Altman, President
P.O. Box 2301
Charleston, WV 25302
766-6396

Appalachian Artists Association
Pat Schumacher, President
P.O. Box 961
Princeton, WV 24740
325-2021 (O)

Appalachian Blacksmiths Association
Boyd Holtan
1257 Dogwood Avenue
Morgantown, WV 26505
599-0231

Appalachian Craftsmen, Inc.
Dorothy Ann Hillen, Director
P.O. Box 559
Barboursville, WV 25504
736-0030 (O)

Beckley Art Group
Edith Toner
600 Johnstown Road
Beckley, WV 25801
253-3868

Cabin Creek Quilts
Brenda DeBoard, Director
Box 383
Cabin Creek, WV 25034
595-3928 (O)

Cedar Lakes Craft Center
c/o Tim Pyles
Cedar Lakes
Ripley, WV 25271
348-0216 (O)

Claymont Artisans Guild
c/o Jack Chromey
Box 112
Charles Town, WV 25414
725-9854 (O) or 725-6848 (H)

Designers Craft Guild
Mildred Atkins
1208 Des Moines Avenue
Morgantown, WV 26505
292-5596 (H)

Evans Run Art Association, Inc.
Nancy Rodig
111 Evans Run Drive
Martinsburg, WV 25401
263-6414 (H)

Fayette Art League
Mrs. Darrell Pennington
P.O. Box 72
Fayetteville, WV 25840
658-4393

Fort New Salem Craft Program
c/o John Randolph
Fort New Salem
Salem, WV 26426
783-5329 (H)

Fort Randolph Artists and Craftsmen Guild
Cathy Pleska, Secretary
Rt. 1, Box 496
Pt. Pleasant, WV 25550
675-2024

Greenbrier Valley Artisans Guild
Mark Fixter, Chairman
RD 2, Box 35A
Alderson, WV 24910
445-2842

League of Independent Artists
Charles Woodyard
146 Circle Drive
Fairmont, WV 26554
363-3657 (H)

Miners Art Group
Andy Willis
439 Park Avenue
South Charleston, WV 25309

Monongahela Valley Arts and Crafts Co-op
c/o Sally Blackwood
P.O. Box 774
Fairmont, WV 26554
366-0175 (H)

Morgantown Arts Associates, Inc.
Ann Campbell
910 W. Park
Morgantown, WV 26505
292-1581 (H)

Morgantown Fiber Council
Susan Elkins
Rt. 10, Box 13
Cobun Creek Road
Morgantown, WV 26505

Mountain Weavers Guild
Karen Bird
236 Terrace Avenue
Elkins, WV 26241
636-7478

P.A.C.T.
c/o Artspace-Charleston
P.O. Box 3943
Charleston, WV 25339
Pat O'Keefe, Artspace Director
342-6598

Pleasants County Art League
Kitty Gorrell
Box 222, Rt. 1
Friendly, WV 26146

Pineville Senior Citizens Co-op
c/o Shirley Bullington, Box 494
Pineville, WV 24874
732-8000, Ext. 203

Rural Arts and Crafts Association
1333 Market Street
P.O. Box 227
Parkersburg, WV 26101
422-5493 (O)

Seneca Trail Artists Guild
Thomas J. Allen, President
P.O. Box 132
Elkins, WV 26241
636-1767 (O) or 636-0856 (H)

Tri-State Arts Association
Linda Tracy, President
128 Jefferson Park Drive
Huntington, WV 25704
736-9453

Upshur Visual Art Guild
Sue Johnston, President
P.O. Box 236
Buckhannon, WV 26201
472-0716 (H)

West Virginia Artists and Crafts Guild
Ene Purre, Executive Director
32½ Capitol Street
Charleston, WV 25301
345-0289 (O)

West Virginia Filmmakers Guild
John Nakashima, President
117 Park Street
Morgantown, WV 26505
293-6511 (O) or 292-7910 (H)

West Virginia Theatre Conference
Alma Bennett
Rt. 3, Box 38-H
Philippi, WV 26416
457-1414 (H) or 457-1700 Ext. 287 (O)

West Virginia Watercolor Society
Dava Dahlgram
32 Suzanne Street
Rt. 1
Washington, WV 26181

Special Projects

Special projects are developed by organizations that present arts projects which occur only one time or annually.

Alpine Heritage Preservation, Inc.
Stephen LaFauci, President
P.O. Box 322
Thomas, WV 26292
259-5638

Augusta Heritage Center
Margo Blevin, Director
Davis and Elkins College
Elkins, WV 26241
636-1900 (O)

Charleston Renaissance Corp.
Terrell Eddins, Staff Director
815 Quarrier Street, Suite 235
Charleston, WV 25301
345-1738

Fine Arts Music Camp
Creative Arts Center, WVU
Morgantown, WV 26506
293-2901 (O)

International Food Festival
Robert Kaminski
4028 Pallisades Drive
Weirton, WV 26062
748-3356

Kanawha Valley Senior Services
John F. McCormick
P.O. Box 268
Charleston, WV 25321
348-0707

Mason County Regional State Farm Museum
Walden F. Roush
2003 Mt. Vernon Avenue
Pt. Pleasant, WV 25550
675-2834 (O) or 675-5737

Parkersburg South High School
Parkersburg High School Drama Festival
Steve Rader (PHS)
2101 Dudley Avenue
Parkersburg, WV 26101
485-7941 (O) or 614-667-3827 (H)

Pearl S. Buck Birthplace Foundation
Michael Dotson, Executive Director
P.O. Box 126
Hillsboro, WV 24946
653-4430

Pricketts Fort Memorial Foundation
David Elkinton, Executive Director
Rt. 3, Pricketts Fort State Park
Fairmont, WV 26554
363-3030 (O) or 296-0565 (H)

Pioneer Days in Pocahontas County
Douglas Durback
700 Second Avenue
Marlinton, WV 24954
799-6569 (H) or 799-4315 (O)

Rhododendron State Outdoor Arts and Crafts Association
Robert Harden, President
429 Highland Avenue
South Charleston, WV 25303
744-4323 (H) or 348-5830 (O)

Stonewall Jackson Heritage Arts and Crafts Jubilee
June Foster, Chairman
Box 446
Jane Lew, WV 26278
884-7228 (H)

West Virginia Black Walnut Festival
Richard L. Gregg, Festival Committee
P.O. Box 77
Spencer, WV 25276
925-3780

West Virginia Public Radio
Richard Eiswerth, Program Operation Manager
Building 6, Room B424
Capitol Complex
Charleston, WV 25305
348-3239 (O) or 343-0555 (H)

West Virginia State Folk Festival
Diane Bach, President
907H Walnut Street
Glenville, WV 26351
462-7361, Ext 224 (O)

Professional Resources

Professional art organizations may provide mailing lists, grants, publications, newsletters, conferences, etc.

Affiliate Artists, Inc.
155 West 68th Street
New York, NY 10023
212-580-2000

Alliance for Arts Education
John F. Kennedy Center for the Performing Arts
Washington, D.C. 20566
202-254-7190

American Arts Alliance
424 C Street, NE
Washington, D.C. 20002
202-544-3900

American Association of Museums
1055 Thomas Jefferson Street, NW
Washington, D.C. 20007
202-338-5300

American Council for the Arts
570 Seventh Avenue
New York, NY 10018
212-354-6655

American Film Institute
Kennedy Center for the Performing Arts
Washington, D.C. 20566
202-828-3400

American Music Center
250 West 54th Street, Room 300
New York, NY 10019
212-247-3121

American Symphony Orchestra League
633 E. Street, NW
Washington, D.C. 20004
202-629-0099

American String Teachers Association
Furman University
Greenville, South Carolina 29613

American Theatre Association
1010 Wisconsin Avenue, NW, 6th Floor
Washington, D.C. 20007
202-342-7530

Art Museum of America
270 Sutter Street
San Francisco, CA 94108
415-397-9222

Association of College, University and Community Arts
Administrators (ACUCAA)
6225 University Avenue
Madison, Wisconsin 53705
608-233-7400

Association of Hispanic Arts
200 East 87th Street
New York, NY 10029
212-369-7054

Association of Independent Video and Filmmakers
625 Broadway
New York, NY 10012
212-473-3400

Association of Professional Vocal Ensembles
251 South 18th Street
Philadelphia, PA 19103
215-545-4444

Back Roads Adventures
(Can arrange for demonstrations and studio visits with
artists and musicians)
Rt. 5, Box 228A
Morgantown, WV 26505
296-0565

Business Committee for the Arts
1775 Broadway, Suite 510
New York, NY 10019
212-664-0600

Center for the Arts Information
625 Broadway
New York, NY 10012
212-677-7548

Center for Occupational Hazards
5 Beekman Street
New York, NY 10038
212-227-6220

Chamber Music America
215 Park Avenue
South 13th Floor
New York, NY 10036
212-460-9030

Corporation for Public Broadcasting
1111 Sixteenth Street, NW
Washington, D.C. 20036
202-293-6160

Dance/USA
633 E Street, NW
Washington, D.C. 20004
202-628-0144

Dramatist Guild
234 W. 44th Street
New York, NY 10036
212-398-9366

**Foundation for the Extension and
Development of American Professional Theatre**
165 W. 47th Street, Suite 310
New York, NY 10036
212-869-9690

Grantsmanship Center, The
1031 South Grad Avenue
Los Angeles, CA 90015
800-421-9512 or 213-749-4721

Humanities Foundation of West Virginia
Charles Daugherty, Executive Director
P.O. Box 204
Institute, WV 25712
304-768-8869

Institute of Museum Services
1100 Pennsylvania, NW
Washington, D.C. 20506
202-426-6577

Mid-Atlantic States Arts Consortium
Suite 7-B
11 East Chase Street
Baltimore, MD 21003
301-685-1400

National Assembly of Local Arts Agencies
1785 Massachusetts Avenue, NW
Suite 413
Washington, D.C. 20036
202-483-8670

National Association of Regional Ballet
1860 Broadway
New York, NY 10023
212-757-8460

National Dance Association
1900 Association Drive
Reston, VA 22091
703-476-3400

National Endowment for the Arts
Henry Willett, Regional Representative
310 North Hull Street
Montgomery, AL 36104
205-264-3797

National Endowment for the Arts
1100 Pennsylvania Ave., N.W.
Washington, D.C. 20506
202-682-5400 (Public Information)

National Endowment for the Humanities
1100 Pennsylvania Ave., N.W.
Washington, D.C. 20506
202-786-0438

National Museum of Women in the Arts
4590 MacArthur Boulevard, N.W.
Washington, D.C. 20007
202-337-2615

Opera America
1010 Vermont Avenue, N.W. #702
Washington, D.C. 20005
202-347-9212

Poets and Writers
201 West 54th Street
New York, NY 10019
212-757-1766

Southeastern Theatre Conference
1209 W. Market Street
Greensboro, NC 27412
919-272-3645

TARTS/Teaching Artists to Reach Technological Savvy
Ariel Dougherty
Women's Studio Workshop
P.O. Box V
Rosendale, NY 12473
914-658-9133

Theatre Communications Group (TCG)
355 Lexington Avenue
New York, NY 10017
212-687-5230

Visual Artists and Galleries Association
141 Fifth Avenue, 6-N
New York, NY 10036
212-575-1150

West Virginia Art Educators Association
Paula Meadows, President
Route 2, Box 82
Milton, WV 25541
304-743-6651 (H) or 304-757-7055 (O)

West Virginia Artists and Craftsmen Guild
Ene Purre, Executive Director
32½ Capitol Street
Charleston, WV 25301
304-345-0289

West Virginia Education Fund
Vivian Kidd, Director
1126 Kanawha Valley Building
Charleston, WV 25301
304-342-7850

West Virginia Music Educators Association
Don Hamilton, President
522 Stout Street
Bridgeport, WV 26330
304-623-2901 (O) or 304-824-3380 (H)

West Virginia Music Teachers Association
Mary Delle Thomas
635 Holly Road
Charleston, WV 25314
304-346-1040

West Virginia String Teachers Association
David Becker, President
1015-11th Avenue
Huntington, WV 25701
304-522-0813 (H)

West Virginia Theatre Conference
Alma Bennett
Rt. 3, Box 38-H
Philippi, WV 26416
457-1414 (H) or 457-1700 (O)

West Virginia Writers, Inc.
Joyce Stover, President
Route 1, Box 163
Given, WV 25245
303-747-2339 (O) or 304-372-3600 (H)

West Virginia University Cooperative Extension Service
(Provides workshops and publications on home-based business, volunteerism clothing and textiles, community development, and management skills, as well the better-known agriculture and home economics skills.)
Knapp Hall
P.O. Box 6031
Morgantown, WV 26506-6031
293-2694
(Or contact your County Extension Office)

West Virginia Filmmakers
John Nakashima
117 Park Street
Morgantown, WV 26505
304-293-6511 (O) or 304-292-7910 (H)

Young Audiences, Inc.
115 East 92nd Street
New York, NY 10028
212-831-8110

Fairs and Festivals

Jackson County's Annual Quilt Show and Sale (April)
Location: North & Church St., Ripley, WV
Sponsor: Jackson County Extension Homemakers
Contact: Sue Black
 P.O. Box 471
 Ripley, WV 25271
 372-2011 Ext. 19

Dogwood Arts and Crafts Festival (April)
Location: Huntington Civic Center
Sponsor: City of Huntington
Contact: P.O. Box 2767
 Huntington, WV 25727
 696-5990

Dogwood Festival (May)
Location: Mullens, WV
Sponsor: Mullens Area Chamber of Commerce
 504 Brammer Street
 Mullens, WV 25882
 294-7484

Blue Ridge Quilt Show (May)
Location: Harpers Ferry, WV
Sponsor: Blue Ridge Quilters
Contact: Kathy Kime
 Rt. 1, Box T-137
 Harpers Ferry, WV 25425

Allegheny Mountain Wool Fair (May)
Location: Allegheny Mountain Wool Fairgrounds
 Mingo-Randolph County
Contact: Donald Wood, President
 Star Route
 Mingo, WV 26281
 339-2659

Heritage Festival (May)
Location: Huntington Galleries
Sponsor: Huntington Galleries
Contact: Gay Jackson
  529-2701

Riverfest (May)
Location: Parkersburg, WV
Sponsor: Fine Arts Council, Wood County
Contact: Fine Arts Council
  P.O. Box 1705
  Parkersburg, WV 26101
  428-3988

West Virginia Strawberry Festival (May/June)
Location: Buckhannon, WV
Sponsor: WV Strawberry Festival Association
Contact: Gary Ogden
  Route 7, Box 94
  Buckhannon, WV 26201
  472-5674

Webster County Woodchopping Festival (May)
Location: Webster Spring, WV
Sponsor: Webster County Woodchopping Festival
Contact: 155 McGraw Avenue
  Webster Springs, WV 26288

Rhododendron Outdoor Arts and Crafts Festival (June)
Location: Charleston, WV
Sponsor: Rhododendron Arts & Crafts Association
Contact: Robert Harden
  429 Highland Avenue
  South Charleston, WV 25303
  744-4323

Mountain Heritage Arts and Crafts Festival (June)
Location: Charles Town, WV
Sponsor: Jefferson County Chamber of Commerce
Contact: George E. Vickers, Manager
  P.O. Box 426
  Charles Town, WV 25414
  725-2055

West Virginia Folk Festival (June)
Location: Glenville, WV
Sponsor: Town of Glenville & Glenville State College
Contact: Mack Samples
  Rt. 78, Box 25
  Linn, WV 26384
  462-7572

Tri-State Fair and Regatta (June)
Location: Huntington, WV
Harris Riverfront Park
Contact: Lisa M. Mahood
  P.O. Box 1643
  Ashland, KY 41105
  606-329-8737

West Virginia Birthday Celebration (June)
Location: Fairmont, WV
Sponsor: Cross Roads Community Center
Contact: Kimberly Slides
  Rt. 4, Box 414
  Fairmont, WV 26554
  363-6160

Farm Festival (June)
Location: Wheeling, WV
Sponsor: Oglebay Good Zoo
Contact: Penny Miller
  c/o Oglebay Good Zoo
  Wheeling, WV 26003
  242-3000

Summersville Bluegrass Country Music Festival (June)
Location: Summersville, WV
Contact: Edgar Kitchen
  P.O. Box 96
  Summersville, WV 26651
  872-3145

Mountain State Arts and Crafts Fair (July)
Location: Cedar Lakes
  Ripley, WV
Sponsor: Mountain State Arts & Crafts Fair
Contact: Steve Vasiliou
  879 Ivy Avenue
  Wheeling, WV 26003
  232-5424

Weirton International Food Fair & Festival (July)
Location: Weirton, WV
Sponsor: Festival Committee
Contact: Chuck Lafferty
  c/o Weirton Steel Corp.
  MAB Annex, 113 Penn. Ave.
  Weirton, WV 26062
  797-3768

Augusta Heritage Arts Workshop (July/August)
Location: Elkins, WV
Sponsor: Davis & Elkins College
Contact: Doug Hall
  Davis & Elkins College
  Elkins, WV 26241
  636-1903

Upper Ohio Valley Italian Festival (July)
Location: Wheeling, WV
Sponsor: Wheeling Area Chamber of Commerce
Contact: Thomas A. Cerra
  21 Armory Drive
  Wheeling, WV 26003
  242-0520

Logan County Arts & Crafts Fair (August)
Location: Logan, WV
Sponsor: Logan County Chamber of Commerce
Contact: Connie White, Director
    Box 218
    313 Huggins St., Suite 20
    Logan, WV 25601
    752-1324

Cherry River Festival (August)
Location: Richwood, Nicholas County
Sponsor: City of Richwood
Contact: Tom Wagner
    P.O. Box 767
    Richwood, WV 26261
    846-2058

Town & Country Days (August)
Location: 4-H Grounds
    New Martinsville, WV
Sponsor: Town & Country Days, Inc.
Contact: Robert Lasure
    P.O. Box 644
    New Martinsville, WV 26155
    455-2928

The Ohio River Festival (August)
Location: Riverfront Park
    Ravenswood, WV
Sponsor: The Ohio River Festival, Inc.
Contact: Wilcie Skaggs, President
    204 Race Street
    Ravenswood, WV 26164
    273-4157

Gospel Sing (August)
Location: Summersville, WV
Contact: Edgar Kitchen
    P.O. Box 96
    Summersville, WV 26651
    872-3145

State Fair of West Virginia (August)
Location: Fairlea, WV
    Greenbrier County
Contact: State Fair of WV
    Lewisburg, WV 24901
    645-1090

Appalachian Arts & Crafts Festival (August)
Location: Raleigh County
Sponsor: Beckley-Raleigh Chamber of Commerce
Contact: William A. Wilbur, Director
    P.O. Box 1798
    Beckley, WV 25802
    252-7328

Charleston Sternwheel Regatta Festival (August)
Location: Charleston, WV
Sponsor: City of Charleston
Contact: Henrietta L. Cook
    P.O. Box 2749
    Charleston, WV 25330
    348-6419

Country Roads Festival (August)
Location: Pennsboro, Ritchie County
Sponsor: Country Roads Festival
Contact: Sondra Hayhurst
    101 Broadway Street
    Pennsboro, WV 26415
    659-2926

West Virginia Bluegrass Festival (August)
Location: Walker, WV
    Cox's Field
Contact: John Cox
    Rt. 1
    Walker, WV 26180
    489-2280

Hilltop Festival (August)
Location: Huntington Galleries
    Huntington, WV
Contact: Gay Jackson
    c/o Huntington Galleries
    Huntington, WV 24701
    529-2701

Stonewall Jackson Heritage Arts & Crafts Jubilee (September)
Location: Jackson's Mill State 4-H Camp
Sponsor: Stonewall Jackson Heritage Arts & Crafts Jubilee
Contact: Peggy Doyle
    Executive Secretary
    P.O. Box 956
    Weston, WV 26452
    269-1863

West Virginia Italian Heritage Festival (September)
Location: Clarksburg, WV
Contact: John S. Manna, Director
    P.O. Box 1632
    Clarksburg, WV 26301
    622-1986

Town of Gauley Bridge Anniversary Festival (September)
Location: Gauley Bridge
    Fayette County
Sponsor: Town of Gauley Bridge
    Box 490
    Gauley Bridge, WV
    632-2504

Summersville Bluegrass-Country Music Festival (September)

Location: Summersville, WV
Contact: Edgar Kitchen
P.O. Box 96
Summersville, WV 26651
872-3145

West Virginia Oil & Gas Festival (September)

Location: Sistersville, WV
Sponsor: West Virginia Oil & Gas Festival Association
Contact: Stewart Bradfield
P.O. Box 25
Sistersville, WV 26175
652-7881

Fort Henry Festival (September)

Location: Wheeling Civic Center
Wheeling, WV
Sponsor: Wheeling Civic Center & Retail Division of the
Chamber of Commerce
Contact: Judy Rowles
#2 14th Street
Wheeling, WV 26003
233-7000

King Coal Festival (September)

Location: Williamson, WV
Sponsor: AIM Group
Contact: Mae Stallard
28 Oak Street
Williamson, WV 25661
135-5560

Arts & Crafts Fall Festival (September)

Location: Alderson Junior High Gym
Sponsor: Alderson Junior Woman's Club
Contact: Karen Lobban
Box 148
Alderson, WV 24910
445-7730

Harvest Moon Festival of Arts and Crafts (September)

Location: Parkersburg, WV
Sponsor: Wood County Fine Arts Council
Contact: Fine Arts Council
P.O. Box 1705
Parkersburg, WV 26101
428-3988

Treasure Mountain Festival (September)

Location: Franklin, WV
Sponsor: Treasure Mountain Festival Association
Contact: Harriet McCoy
Box 336
Franklin, WV 26807
358-2275

Craigsville Fall Festival (September)

Location: Craigsville, WV
Contact: Craigsville, WV 26205
742-3489

Country Road Festival (September)

Location: Hawk's Nest State Park
Ansted, WV
Sponsor: Ansted Lion's Club
Contact: Robert Wilson
Box 537
Ansted, WV 25812
658-4407 or 658-4910

West Virginia Molasses Festival (September)

Location: Arnoldsburg, WV
Sponsor: West Fork Community Action, Inc.
Contact: Deward Offutt
Arnoldsburg, WV 25234
655-8374

Preston County Buckwheat Festival (September)

Location: Kingwood, WV
Sponsor: Kingwood Volunteer Fire Department
Contact: Lucille H. Crogan
111 Beverly Street
Kingwood, WV 26537
329-0021

Fall Mountain Heritage Arts & Crafts Festival (September)

Location: Charles Town, WV
Sponsor: Jefferson County Chamber of Commerce
Contact: George E. Vickers, Manager
P.O. Box 426
Charles Town, WV 25414
725-2055

Poca Area Heritage Day (September)

Location: Poca, Putnam County
Sponsor: Poca Heritage Committee
Contact: Sheila Williamson
P.O. Box 517
Poca, WV 25159
755-4677

Hardy County Heritage Weekend (September)

Location: Moorefield, WV
Sponsor: Hardy County Tour & Craft Association
Contact: Marjorie Zirk
Box 301
Moorefield, WV 26836
538-6560

West Virginia Honey Festival (September)

Location: Parkersburg City Park
Parkersburg, WV
Sponsor: West Virginia Beekeepers Association
City of Parkersburg
Contact: Parkersburg/Wood County Visitors &
Convention Bureau
P.O. Box 2149
Parkersburg, WV
428-1130

Rupert County Fling (September)
    Location: Rupert, WV
    Sponsor: Rupert Area Improvement Co.
    Contact: Jeanne Brenneman
      Route 2, Box 36A
      Rupert, WV 25984
      392-5525

Mountain State Forest Festival (September)
    Location: Elkins, WV
    Contact: Pauline Brooks
      P.O. Box 369
      Elkins, WV 26241
      636-1824

West Virginia Black Walnut Festival (October)
    Location: Spencer, WV
    Contact: West Virginia Black Walnut Festival
      Terry A. Williams
      207 Court
      Spencer, WV 25226
      927-1640

Apple Butter Festival (October)
    Location: Berkeley Springs State Park
      Berkeley Springs, WV
    Sponsor: Berkeley Springs-Morgan County
      Chamber of Commerce
    Contact: Andrea Beth Peters
      204 N. Washington Street
      Berkeley Springs, WV 25411
      258-3738

Mountain State Apple Harvest Festival
    Location: West Virginia Air National Guard Building
      Martinsburg, WV
    Sponsor: Mountain State Apple Harvest Festival, Inc.
    Contact: Nancy Rodig
      P.O. Box 1362
      Martinsburg, WV 25401
      263-2500 or 263-6414

Carol Bryan Recommends . . .

The Art of Creative Thinking: A Practical Guide, Robert W. Olson (Barnes and Noble, 1980). How to nurture, develop and exercise creative abilities. Illustrated.

The Dynamics of Creation, Anthony Storr (Penguin, revised 1983). A fascinating inquiry into why artists and scientists engage in creative activity.

The Creative Process, Brewster Ghiselin (Mentor, 1952). Creativity explained by 38 geniuses including Einstein, Van Gogh, Thomas Wolfe, Mozart, Amy Lowell and others.

Creativity: The Magic Synthesis, Silvano Arieti (Basic Books, 1976). Author shows, with scientific exactitude, that creativity is a gift given in greater or lesser measure, but that its expression cannot occur without effort and support.

Higher Creativity: Liberating the Unconscious for Breakthrough Insights, Willis Harmon and Howard Rhiengold (Tarcher, 1984). Teaches how to have the creative "breakthrough experience" frequently through shedding thoughts of limitation and self-doubt.

On Not Being Able to Paint, Joanna Field (Tarcher, 1957). Could as easily have been called On Not Being Able to Write . . . Compose . . . Dance . . . Think . . . Create. Excites and challenges anyone eager to learn about the nature of the creative process, when it flourishes . . . and does not.

The Drama of the Gifted Child, Alice Miller (Basic Books, 1981). How narcissistic parents form and deform the emotional lives of their talented children.

Invented Worlds: The Psychology of the Arts, Ellen Winner (Harvard Press, 1982). A vast array of research on creativity, combined with developmental psychology of the arts. What impels the artist (writer, musician) to the lonely effort of self-expression, what moves audiences to respond, and more.

Working It Out, ed. Sara Ruddick and Pamela Daniels (Pantheon, 1977). 23 women writers, artists, scientists and scholars talk about their lives and work.

Staying Power, Peter Barton (The Dial Press, 1980). Twelve performing artists talk about the struggle, pain, setbacks, emotional aspects, politics, excitement and satisfaction of surviving against great odds and fierce competition in their respective fields.

Particular Passions, Lynn Gilbert and Gaylen Moore (Potter, 1981). Talks with 46 women who have shaped our times. Includes sculptor Louise Nevelson, writers Lillian Hellman and Alice Walker, choreographer Agnes DeMille, chef Julia Child, conductor Sarah Caldwell.

Becoming a More Creative Person, John A. Glover (Prentice-Hall, 1980). Using self-management to develop greater creativity in writing, problem-solving and interpersonal skills.

Rejection, John White (Addison-Wesley, 1982). Thoroughly researched and well-presented collection of often-amusing material dealing with "rejection," to which all creators can relate.

Visualization: Directing the Movies of Your Mind, Adelaide Bry (Barnes and Noble, 1978). How to improve your health, expand your mind, increase your creativity and achieve your life goals.

The Art of Creative Thinking, Gerard I. Nierenberg (Cornerstone Library, 1982). A system of step-by-step methods for realizing greater creativity and mental capability.

The Courage to Create, Rollo May (Norton, 1975). A stimulating exploration of the power of creativity. The discovery of new forms, symbols and patterns on which society can be built.

Culture, Crisis and Creativity, Dane Rudhyar (Quest, 1977). "There comes a time we should consider breaking away from established patterns and values that have been imposed upon us through our culture."

Imagineering: How to Profit From Your Creative Powers, Michael LeBoeuf (McGraw-Hill, 1980). Methods, exercises, techniques which encourage greater creativity.

The Mind's Best Work, D.N. Perkins (Harvard Press, 1981). A witty, guided tour of the new psychology of creative thinking. Considered one of the current "bests."

Passion for the Piano, Judith Oringer (Tarcher, 1983). A richly illustrated medley of history, practical advice, and the personal accounts of performers, teachers, and judges; anecdotes from superstar pianists which reveal their inspiration to continue playing, practicing and performing. Complete and delightful.

Elegy for a Soprano (Fiction), Kay Nolte Smith (Villard, 1985). An uncompromising look at the dark side of the prima donna personality. Not a false note.

Creative Person Magazine - indepth interviews with creators, supportive and educational articles of interest to those who are serious about their creativity. Issues #1, #2, #3 & #4 are available for $3.00 each. All four issues for $10.00 from Carol Bryan Imagines, 1000 Byus Drive, Charleston, WV 25311.

"The Courage to Create" - two 60-minute cassette tapes from the award-winning NPR documentary. Numerous artists, musicians, writers and others explore their thoughts about the creative process.

The New York Times (particularly Sunday): Always filled with timely information and inspiration for any creator. (Especially the Arts & Leisure section, and Book Review and often the Magazine). Worth a subscription.

Artist's Market (Writer's Digest, Cincinnati, Ohio. Annual). Lists publishers — what they publish and how to submit your work to them; consumer publication; trade, technical and professional journals, etc. Available at almost every public library.

Fiction Writer's Market (Writer's Digest, Cincinnati, Ohio. Annual). How and where to get your short stories and novels published. Available at most public libraries.

Guide to Women's Art Organizations and Directory for the Arts, Cynthia Navaretta (Midmarch Associates, 1982). Help with everything from funding to artist's colonies.

Literary Marketplace (R.R. Bowker, New York. Annual). Lists everything from book publishers to literary agents to editorial and art services to mailing list brokers and much more. Available at most public libraries in the reference section.

National Directory of Shops/Galleries/Shows/Fairs (Writer's Digest, Cincinnati, Ohio. Annual). Where to exhibit and sell your work: drawings, glasswork, weaving, photography, sculpture, leatherwork, metalsmithing, needlework, pottery, oil paintings, basketry, watercolors.

Contributors

Nancy Abrams is a staff photographer for the *Dominion Post* of Morgantown. She lives in Terra Alta in rural Preston County.

Gail Galloway Adams is completing a doctorate in American Studies from Emory University. A former dancer, she now writes. Her fiction and poetry has appeared in *The American Voice,* the *Georgia Review,* and the *North American Review.*

Maggie Anderson writes poetry and shares generously with her students from her home base in Waynesburg, Pennsylvania. She is a frequent teacher for such programs as Elderhostel, art centers, and Poet-in-the Schools. Her most recent book is *Cold Comfort,* a collection of poetry published by the University of Pittsburgh Press.

Ruth Frazier majored in philosophy and minored in literature, but has spent a lifetime reading, teaching, and writing in women's studies. After 21 years at Hollins College in Virginia, she has recently become Director of Adult and Continuing Education at Endicott College in Massachusetts.

Mary Lynn Ganahl, a stained glass hobbyist, is a contributing editor for *Victorian Poetry* at West Virginia University. She is married to a family therapist and is the mother of a five-year-old son.

Sharon Goodman, artist, dancer, researcher, and woman of many talents, works at the West Virginia Women's Commission in Charleston.

Betty Donley Harris of Morgantown writes, "Now in my widowed sixties I am trying to write and I know this is something I have always wanted to do."

Marianne Jahnke, a postdoctoral fellow in biochemistry at West Virginia University, is also a folk dancer and an amateur dulcimer performer.

Martha Bibby Miles, originally from New York, has settled happily into West Virginia. An instructor and tutor at West Virginia University, she is the mother of three children and is a poet.

Ann E. Miller, originally from Oregon, is a reference librarian at West Virginia University. When not answering questions, she is likely to be reading, knitting, going to the theatre, or "watching too much TV."

Judy Mattson Reed studied clay at Glenville State College. As a teacher in public schools with two small daughters, she found little time or energy for clay. Now she teaches art at Salem College and produces pottery for craft shows.

Sharon Santos, a graduate of the University of the Pacific, is a professional tutor in the Writing Laboratory at West Virginia University. She is a wife and a mother of two grown sons.

Diane Schwenker, of Huntington, taught college-level classes in drawing, painting, and aesthetic theory. She was an expert photographer, spinner, and weaver who until her death in October 1983 operated her own graphic design business. Her varied interests—folk art, primitives, naives and visionaries, and wild flowers and butterflies—are discernible in her work.

Rosemary Serian is a busy free-lance artist living in Westover. Her art teacher at one time was Sharon Goodman.

Jo Silman, a Wood County native, lives at "Heather Hills Farm" in Roane County. As an Arts Advocate, she has worked extensively to promote West Virginia arts and crafts, hosting the TV program "Lively Arts," writing for and speaking on WV Public Radio, and serving as President of the West Virginia Artists and Craftsmens Guild. She received the "Citizen of the Year" award from the WV Chapter of the Public Relations Society of America in 1986.

Cheryl Torsney owns two quilts, a "Drunkard's Path," pieced and quilted by Dorothy Swonger in Ohio, and a "Greek Cross," pieced and quilted by Lucille Sojourner in the Mississippi State Penitentiary. She lives in Morgantown where she teaches English at West Virginia University and cares for her new baby Benjamin.

Susan Williams of Oak Hill is a fiction writer with "a few pieces published." She is a staff writer for the Charleston *Gazette*.

Linda Yoder lives near Morgantown on a lovingly-restored farm, Owl Creek Farm. She teaches English at Salem College.

●